Refreshing the Customer Dialogue –
with Personalization, Teaching and Algorithms

MATTIAS SJOVALL

Refreshing the Customer Dialogue – with Personalization, Teaching and Algorithms

The Cassiopeia Method – a Practical Guide and
Inspiration for Sales, Marketing and Consultancy

Illustration: Moonred Media
Editorial and proof reading: The British Institute, Stockholm –
Sheila MacDonald-Rannström M.Ed.
Copyright © Mattias Sjövall 2018
Printing: BoD – Books on Demand, Stockholm, Sweden
Production: BoD – Books on Demand, Norderstedt, Germany
Layout: BoD – Books on Demand
ISBN: 978-91-7699-987-5

TABLE OF CONTENTS

INTRODUCTION

THE HOOK – BE THE BRIGHT SHINING STAR FOR YOUR CUSTOMERS

You and the Customer.

A room full of expectations, ambition, coffee and a fog of common distractions; mobile updates and last-minute laptop typing.

And an upcoming *Customer Dialogue.*

And as some version of a customer representative; Account Executive, Consultant, Key Account Manager, Business Developer, you have done this a thousand times before and you are confident about delivering the pitch and all kinds of basic answers to questions the customer will probably come up with, except for the special and highly complicated ones. But then you simply propose a new and prepared meeting with all the answers you might need, or even bring a skilled colleague to that meeting. All good.

It's just that – things have changed. Everything has changed. The customer expects something totally different.

Nevertheless, routinely you start going through given facts, already known by the customer.

Hey, you can skip that, I already know that.

You are used to that response. No problem, objection handling is in your DNA, you just pick up the pace and articulate the simple facts to make them sound a bit more sophisticated.

Hey, really, please tell me something I don't already know. It took me three minutes before this meeting to google all that you have now told me.

Hard stop, and you are not prepared for this. Additionally, you're now really regretting you didn't bring a specialist colleague along for this meeting. But this was just meant to be high-level, a first meeting, an exploratory meeting, the customer talking, not me. This is what you do and have always done.

This is the big change. The character of this meeting, and the expectations.

The phase before the first conversational meeting, the truly first phase in the customer journey, where the customer becomes aware of both the problem and a few potential brand solutions. And collects basic facts about the vendors, product descriptions and market trends – that phase and job is already history for the customer when entering the first vendor meeting. A customer has it all at their fingertips, probably updated a few minutes before the meeting or been researching for weeks. The digital world pays off. The customer expects to meet a specialist in the first meeting. Actually, at every meeting.

Yes, we know this, but what do we do about it?

Additionally, Content Marketing thrives in providing customers with facts and stories before the first face-to-face meeting between the customer and vendor.

But really, what happens when the customer meets the vendor in real life? It doesn't matter if it is Business-to-Business (B2B) or Business-to-Consumer (B2C) – the expectation is something else; and the customer demands soon go through the roof, the sky is no limit anymore and we need to do things totally differently.

A customer meets with a vendor to have the complex and unclear parts explained, in their context, *personalized*, filled with wisdom, best practice and future predictions. It has become a much tougher world for vendors, and this is what *Refreshing The Customer Dialogue* is about.

As a vendor, how do you pull this off?

There are potential pitfalls like a *disconnected understanding* or a possible *attention challenge*. And for the vendor; the topic is suddenly considered fairly complicated and you need to be brilliant to win a smile.

How to be relevant and interesting while delivering a business message with this demanding customer?

It's all about conducting a customer meeting and in the conversation explaining and clarifying a complex matter. How to instantly create trust in a customer-facing situation by teaching what is potentially unclear to make it clear? And how to align the communication in a personalized way.

You as a vendor will be appreciated and stand out in the competition if you do this well.

It's about *teaching the complex*.

And eventually seeing the customer cheer up right there in front of you and honestly thanking you for enlightening them.

Sounds like magic, I just call it The Cassiopeia Method.

And as for all good skills, it takes practice to master this. I can provide the instructions and equip anyone who wants to learn this with enough tools to succeed.

But at the same time, I'm not naive, I believe *my approach is only one way* among a multitude of other possible techniques and skills, but The Cassiopeia Method is tangible, it is here and offers a good start. Hopefully you'll find parts of it or all of it useful.

Although, the most critical part of all this is obviously to understand this big shift in customer and vendor behavior and do something about it. And if nothing else, it will create and inspire a better world for the customers and additionally we'll level up the professional practice of sales, marketing and consultancy.

You won't find the term The Cassiopeia Method in any scientific papers or business literature with publication date prior to this book, because the term comes from me and the name is there for good reasons.

The essence of The Cassiopeia Method is my distilled experience, insights and continually personalized great feedback from customers and students. It's built on twenty years of sales & marketing practice, consultancy, university studies, management and teaching. I have been mainly active in the commercial and highly complex Software Technology industry, but I also have years of experience from the classroom format in state schools teaching kids.

There a basically two unique factors when it comes to The Cassiopeia Method; firstly, it is the extreme interest in the receiver of the communication, how you *see* that person, and secondly it is about using the right *perspectives* when delivering the teaching. In addition to that, a precondition but hardly unique, is the engagement and level of understanding required in the specific topic you will teach.

Nevertheless, it's fundamental and also a critical component of The Cassiopeia Method.

I recommend engaging and trying to fully understand the reasons for the overall change in the New Customer Dialogue, because then you will be able to fully implement a new approach in your unique context, and not only mechanically deliver a new communication technique.

You should be prepared and professional but it is important to realize that we are preparing for a moment's interaction with a *human being*, and then anything can happen, and it all happens instantly, in the moment. It is key to improve your skills in delivering in present time and this is the cornerstone when you take the customer and student, virtually, by the hand and bring them on a learning journey to explore the complex matter you need to explain to them. There are simple tools and techniques in The Cassiopeia Method to help you as a commercially driven teacher to clarify and make the customer follow you all the way into the darkest dungeons and then out into the light on the other side of the story. Get to know expectation management, an executive summary format, story journeys, zoom in and zoom out, in-flow repetition, the Swedish perspective, play intelligence, digital curation etc.

The customer becomes your student and disciple for a moment.

This works so well because you *see* the customer as a holistic human being and you put everything in the right *perspective*. And in the right perspective for the customer, not for you. Keep up the ambition of constant personalization.

You should be able to do this in your normal conversation during a customer meeting. A natural and built-in-way of leading a value-driven discussion forward.

The one-on-one meeting is the primary use case for this, but all the same, this method is as useful for marketers creating marketing content and who aim to offer clarity in the market category, building an Audience and provide appreciated pieces of information.

And it's just as usable for professional keynote speakers or classroom teachers. When you are on stage at your speaking gig, or simply being a teacher in front of a group of customers and students.

You are not selling what you are selling, directly.

You are earning Trust.

Eventually, you might sell something. That would obviously be proof of the success, since we are doing all this with commercial intent and objectives.

But the main direct and first objective, and result, of The Cassiopeia Method is to earn Trust.

Because when you have earned Trust from the customer, only imagination sets the limit for a prosperous relationship. And the teaching becomes part of a commercial context and you give yourself a chance to do business with a much more satisfied customer.

You create a better Customer Experience.

Ultimately, this is part of a huge shift in the way we look at and execute a *Customer Dialogue*. Let us together keep designing a somewhat new and improved world of Sales, Marketing and Consultancy – to new levels of quality and appreciation. Enlighten, clarify and teach the complex, exactly what the Customer is so desperately asking for.

Welcome to the world of the Cassiopeia Stars.

ENLIGHTENMENT CREATES BEAUTIFUL CUSTOMER EXPERIENCES

Let me tell you a story.

Picture *her*; brown hair, middle-aged, she has been working in an office environment for many years, holds a university degree, considered likeable and yes, she is definitely someone you would want on your team, and let us call her *Eve*.

And we've also got *him*; the determined male, short cut hair, maybe some hints of grey, also middle-aged, sometimes in a suit, always wearing a shirt, always having been loyal about how things have been managed in the past and he is eager to keep most parts as-is or at least be a strong influencer of minor changes, we'll call him *Adam*.

They both operate in quite a common office environment. You would recognize it.

However, they are both considered smart and well educated and do what is needed to keep up; obviously professionally at work but also basically in most aspects of life. In fact, as human beings living in times of immense intellectual maturity, privileged with work, food on the table and a good night's sleep in a normal and pretty peaceful part of the world – their whole future lies in their hands. They might realize it at some level or in some aspects but they have never carved out time or created mental space to consider and truly assimilate the width and depth of it and they might not dare to address it too seriously because then they would probably begin to make bad decisions. And obviously, they don't want that. Never ever make bad decisions! And in this case, they know they will do exactly that, end up with bad decisions, and that is an understandable and prudent conclusion considering the magnitude of it all and their view of themselves and the lack of trust in their own ability to understand what is going on.

They honestly don't know what to do about the future, and this all leads them to the point that they suddenly would really appreciate someone else with the ability to guide them, coming up with suggestions, providing them with some healthy nudges towards the best version of the future, best practice and wisdom. A way and direction that make them stay on course perfectly aligned to where the world and their colleagues and friends are heading, but still making them a little bit unique as individuals. Eventually, Adam and Eve become very open minded about being influenced by whoever's out there and communicating with enough trust and credibility, telling them what to do and whatever decision that needs to be made. Teaching them.

Teaching and clarifying the complex aspects of business and life.

Adam and Eve might have been born with names with impressive similarity to their predecessors in the creation myth, but they more or less immediately and secretly decided that the names should be the only similarity. Period. But now, in this context of important future decisions and different roads to choose, they need to agree that in the position they find themselves, it is a little bit the same as for the first versions of Adam and Eve. What do they do with the future and everything that seems to have been created for them? Actually, they don't know how but it even feels like they have become the creators of the undefined future days to come.

Their response to all this turns out to be what they usually do: they send out invitations to an internal meeting at nine o'clock on Thursday morning next week. The invited lucky ones are the team they belong to and their manager and this time also the manager's manager and they label the meeting: *The future is ours – we create it and this is where we decide to go.*

Well, to be honest, that headline made both their manager and his manager a little bit worried. However, Adam and Eve of course expected that and their intention was to have full attendance at the meeting because now when they had gained this new insight of the white space future, and the lack of concrete suggestions on how to play it right, they couldn't hold back anymore, it was time to discuss, reflect and do something about it, and do it together. And the more thought they put into this the closer they came to a proposed approach to the future, and they were eager to maintain the pace. Normally the managers would have done what they could to cancel this meeting and take the discussion offline, but both managers were ten plus years younger than Adam and Eve and this time the new creators were decisive, you could feel it in the air in the office, you could smell it, above the cold coffee, too much perfume and someone heating up a chicken lunch in the kitchen area.

The worst problem they had on the other hand was that they had so few ideas around what to present or how to lead the discussion forward. The reason was that they realized they didn't really understand the world. Just parts of it. And it wasn't getting any easier in an era of technology with new complicated products and solutions overwhelming them every day with new features, mobile apps, real-time services and even artificial intelligence – whatever that meant? And if Adam and Eve, not even them, two ambitious and fast learning human beings didn't understand, who did? Engineers, space scientists, monks? For sure, engineers understood technology, and analysts might describe companies with people's and society's new behaviors, and humanists can depict the complex human beings in an historical perspective, and business managers and politicians know all about individuals hungry for power and appreciation. But holistically, who did really understand the new world of technology, real time economy and human beings that are both updated and not updated? Maybe *this* was the core for the new approach?

Adam and Eve looked at each other after that reflection. They concluded that they needed a lunch snack with an extra cup of coffee, a walk outside the office building, maybe an ice cream on top of that.

We need more people who can really explain, teach and put things in the right context.

And if we need it, it is highly probable that others need it too.

In essence, clarifying the conditions of the world today. At least situational, where it makes sense for me. There are not a lot people who could do that well, Adam and Eve argued, but at least, in a company context, as a vendor with customers, anyone should be able to shed some light on how they were positioned, what their company actually can solve for their customers, *explain and teach what you are doing and providing.* So that people could really understand. *Really.* And wouldn't the customers appreciate it like they never have appreciated a vendor? Finally be able to offer the great customer experience everyone is talking about but having such a hard time delivering on. That was the only sensible conclusion they could come up with. If we see more of this kind of best practice, a lot more, then in total we might see tendencies towards creating a different world. In this Era of Technology, we need clarity; we need to understand to make better decisions. But since we are proud people, and sometimes scared to not appear updated and intellectual enough, and Adam and Eve nod their heads as they arrive at this over their lunch walk, we often end up in situations where no one in the room dares to ask the obvious questions, but most of us need to slow down and get things straightened out before proceeding.

After their ice cream, they had also clarified how to initiate this transformation process; to start where they were, at the company where Adam and Eve worked and knew every aspect of. They realized that the least they could do was to open up for a much more clarified picture and crystal-clear story for their customers. At least Adam and Eve shouldn't leave any confused souls behind after this. Everyone should be enlightened, and we should not stop educating them on our products, we should keep helping our customers to understand more than that, we should help them understand our whole industry, how it all fits together and how they should navigate their way through it! And why even stop there? Let's position ourselves and the customers in the perspectives of the Universe!

The next Thursday morning during the meeting Adam and Eve were all fired up and they saw open mouths and colleagues staring and listening to them laying out the words, far broader than their job description asked them to do, here's basically what they said:

Team, we have come to a point where the concrete communication and interaction through Sales, Marketing, Consultancy and Customer Service probably should be more influenced by teaching and learning.

That might be the best customer investments you ever imagined. At least if you want to reach out and attract new customers and re-engage existing customers. Honestly, we have a trust issue in the business world. Customers hesitate to engage and trust a vendor because of a long history of too much marketing and sales manipulation and seduction. This has all lead to a world full of mysterious customers, hidden behind walls and voice mails, hard to even see and sometimes vendors are not really sure if a customer even exists based on the silence. However, many times over the years, the vendors still come out well, and on occasion continue to dictate the rules and the framework. We are all aware of that, and most of us also see something new coming, we can recognize some fundamental changes in the power balance between a customer and a vendor. The customer of today has instant access to all imaginable products and price information and in addition to that; the vendor competition has become global and hyper-intense. The customer gets to decide to a much broader extent now, it's just as simple as that. The vendors finally need to truly please and help out. Service and customer experience have become everything. At the same time this is all happening at a time in which we have never witnessed a more educated and insightful population on Earth; smarter and eager to learn and advance. Add to this the muddled mix we apparently also live in times of complex systems and technology creeping under our skin and infiltrating all corporate and government structures, not to mention the individual human being. The world today is more complicated to understand than ever. Nonetheless, people long for understanding, to make great decisions, privately and in their work. But how can they keep up, understand every part of life, see how things are connected? Well, we google more than ever, and we outsource our lives and companies in order to let a specialist do the job. But what if someone could just tell me how things really work? Or at least the parts that interest and concern me today. But this needs to take place in small doses, consumable, and sorry to say, it definitely needs to be presented in a simple way because my head is full of other stuff, I am not interested in getting a university degree in every aspect of life, just enough understanding to make a decision I am comfortable with. No pressure.

This is where teaching could help instead of solely sales pitching. Or marketing based on education instead of mainly disturbing or sharing millions of content pieces. From a specific perspective, aligned to the individual customer's state of mind, in a very short summarized format, as a journey, this approach will take the individual on a learning trip that should end up with a smile and a higher degree of understanding. That is something a modern company can give to people, prospects and customers for free, to elaborate around their topics of expertise. And when that is done properly, the mysterious customer steps out of the shadow and starts with at least giving out their email address for the next marketing initiative and might even want to talk to you about a specific solution to their unique issues. This approach should be a way to offer a truly appreciated Sales, Marketing, Consultancy and Customer Service.

We offer *trust* and *enlightenment*.

Adam and Eve could tell by the response at the meeting that they were onto something fresh and right, and they both agreed that they had got the basics for Why this was the right path to take and also parts of What to do, although they were not too comfortable with How to do it. To start in practice they would appreciate some guidance on how to embrace this way of working and acting, with some concrete techniques and probably get to develop a few new skills.

We thank Adam and Eve for introducing us to the topic.

The need for practical guidance and ideas around successful best practice on how to integrate teaching and learning in a commercial setup, how to use it as a tool both for the vendor and indirectly for the customer in a modern and updated *teacher style*. That was the very reason for writing this book.

Because of the huge need and customer demand: to be able and skilled enough to take the Customer Dialogue to the next level.

A challenge with this value-driven communication practice is the divergence between understanding the teaching concept description and how to actually execute on it. Marketers have done Content Marketing for years and argue they've always had aspects of education and teaching built in to their marketing tactics. And seasoned Sales Representatives argue they have always educated their customers, for free, on new products and market trends. Partly true, but many times the teaching is not real teaching, it is more marketing of content pieces with a lot of explanations included. Indirectly promoting features, providing insights into different digital formats, and teaching is more of Sales pitches with a teacher's voice rather than anything else.

This creates a tremendous opportunity for brands that can offer a real voice as a Teacher in the market place, and I know what the customer appreciation looks like, and I assure that is something all vendors want.

Although, to design this practice so that it actually works takes skills and tools. Because quality requirements are tougher and customer impatience greater than ever, and a poor performance might keep the customers in the shadow and then they'll continue to ignore you. But with the right tone, touch and interest in both the topic and the customer – you open up for new opportunities.

This book is not primarily about all the instructional videos we see out there; about how to replace a lightbulb or learn how to play the guitar. I love them, but this time we are aiming for the more complicated things in business life like; Technology, Finance, Industrial Products etc. Complex industries. And how you actually frame and present parts and topics *while teaching during a conversation with a customer.* The appreciated dialogue.

Micro-training in the moment. How to clarify and enlighten in a meeting.

Obviously, this would be extra helpful not only for complex industries and established companies but also in particular for startup companies trying to pitch and explain how good, effective and new their unique products or services are. The fact is, the first and most important part is that the customer even understands the context and if a company can meet their needs and challenges. This method I present, The Cassiopeia Method, or some other version of a teaching approach, would be great to see as the obvious best practice for companies in complex industries.

Let us start with some examples of how this could look.

TWO ILLUSTRATIVE EXAMPLES

Case 1 – a vendor's sales representative having a customer face-to-face meeting.

The Sales rep Mark Wilson has, after months of trying, finally got the potential Customer to agree to a lunch for "open discussions" about the industry's latest development. For the Customer, it is really an open discussion although the company he works for has a list of challenges they need to address in the next coming years, just as every company has lists of challenges. For Mark Wilson, this meeting would be about finding business opportunities from that list of challenges that he can match to a product and solution he can eventually sell. Same old prospecting strategy. His company invents products that match each individual human being's "coffee profile" to specific drink offerings in the coffee house, all based on Artificial Intelligence.

Also, this face-to-face lunch meeting is basically a start for building a relationship for the future, and Mark is painfully aware of the competition and the Customer probably doesn't have any problem with paid lunches every week.

Here is the dialogue:

"The fish is what they usually recommend here", says Mark Wilson looking around the restaurant, his favorite place and now with the top prospect finally in front of him.

"Is that so?" The Customer doesn't look impressed at all, unclear if the reason is the minimal lunch menu or Mark's unsolicited recommendation. Probably both.

"I am delighted and I truly appreciate that we could make it eventually, the lunch I mean. I am curious about your situation and hopefully I can share something interesting and valuable that you can bring home too."

Mark would be considered a senior Sales Representative after years of successful selling, he knows pretty well how to talk to a customer, even when they kept their distance. Although today he planned to try another approach. Usually, after the sweet talk he somehow moves onto the topic and digs around trying all the tricks he knows to identify the customer's most urgent problems and at the same time make sure that they get some input into what is happening in the industry, new trends, and what other customers are up to. And hopefully, the lunch meeting ends up in a few follow-up actions leading them forward with one or several concrete business opportunities. Unfortunately, on some occasions, there are no opportunities for such matches at the present time and he needs to check again in six months. Today he was inspired by another approach.

"I am ready to order, I'll go for the meat", says the Customer. He looks tired. Mark's experience tells him that the Customer has something, a need or pressing issue, matching Mark's area of expertise, otherwise they wouldn't agree to being there with him. This was not the kind of customer that was looking for free lunches, this is work for him and something he has to do; endure one hour with a sales person.

"Perfect, I'll stick to the fish, hold on and I'll let them know we are ready to order."

While completing the order Mark swiftly goes over in his head what he prepared earlier. Firstly, Mark already knew his topic, his area of expertise, from top to bottom. He knew all the main aspects of it, the relationships, the larger context, the best practice and the pros and cons. He could have educated an eight-year-old child on this complicated topic; simply and clear. Secondly, and this was a huge difference from prior meetings, he had done an immense amount of research on the person sitting in front of him in the restaurant. By preparing and trying to find out everything there was to know about this person, his career, education, how other people would describe him, articles on the web. Whatever there was to know. And his formal role and title provided information too, what kind of challenges his role in the organization typically faces, basic "marketing persona descriptions", and what kind of company culture he represented, what their company objectives and vision were. Mark was trying to frame, understand and find out all he could about this person. But that was not enough, everyone can do that, although a sales rep might not prioritize it every time, but the big analysis took place in the restaurant. There and then. He initiated a scan from the very beginning when they met in which Mark made some thorough *observations of the person joining him for lunch. The emotions today, potential irritation, happiness, stress, is he tired or longing for something else, something that was pressuring him? Most importantly: where was the customer's mind and thoughts in that exact moment. Because that would be the starting point for Mark. Today he sees a distracted person who probably had too much of negative aspects mastering his mind at the moment. Also, most likely an experienced senior's attitude with a lack of patience and no time for small talk or platitudes. Mark had seen it all before. But intended to treat it differently and as a unique moment.*

"Mr. Anderson, let's do this in a straightforward way, and let's begin already now before they serve the food, they are actually quite fast here. There are things happening on my side of the business that I thought might be interesting/exciting for you to be aware of. I have already given up the thought of selling anything to you since you give the impression of not wanting to be sold to and will most probably make any decision you make based on reasonable facts and not shiny sales pitches, so let's skip that for today."

"Yes, you are right about that!"

The Customer might not yet be on the hook but Mark is receiving continuous acknowledgements during their conversation. As part of his strategy, he wants to lead the Customer forward. Not by manipulation, just though an open journey, discovering areas of common interest, otherwise there is no need to engage in this professional relationship.

"Let me paint you a picture of what I have seen in my part of the business lately, it is quite surprising, so would you excuse me if I just briefly explain to you what a Coffee Island of Artificial Intelligence is?"

"Go ahead, I am just waiting for my meat, and I hear about AI all the time, not sure everyone knows what they are talking about though, and that kind of science fiction technology is for sure nothing for our company at the moment,, but the coffee angle was new, I'll give you that."

Mark notices a few good signs, this is a person who would prefer to truly understand the new products coming, the one's on everyone's lips. Skeptical, yes, but open to gaining new insights, but wouldn't admit it openly.

"Artificial Intelligence is actually not as complicated as many people make it out to be. It's basically an ambition to copy some of the great functions of a human being's mind, pumped up with some super com-

*puter's power and data. Simplified, yes, but all the same the truth.
Provide a machine with a huge amount of situational data and let it
digest it and come up with a judgement, a probability plot, suggestions
for next actions. Everything based of what it learned from previous and
similar situations, represented by huge amounts of data, or a model and
a predicted outcome. Let me put it in a coffee context, if I may?"*

*"That's what I am waiting for, except for the meat, and I guess you
lost me on situational data and probability plots..."*

*"Yes, I appreciate that. Let me clarify. Although, it's surprising how
much information you can derive from a small coffee bean. As crazy as
it might sound, we have carried out analyzes and scans of fifty (!) different coffee beans, the most common ones, and build up an impressive
database of knowledge on what the beans consist of and how that affects
taste, smell and consistence."*

"Okay…"

*"We have it all collected and structured, ready to be used. That is
one important cornerstone to make this AI-solution work – A LOT of
relevant data."*

"Okay…"

*"But that is not enough, you know what, exactly the same coffee is not
only affected by what water it's made with. It's also how the barista and
coffee machine are working individually and together, and even more
interestingly, and this is the new part; Coffee tastes different depending
on circumstances around and inside the consumer. No one seem to have
been thinking about this, busy in inventing new coffee drinks and con-
structing the perfect cup of coffee. All the parameters around the human
being tasting coffee; age, gender, biological preconditions, maybe he or
she has just eaten something, still with that taste in their mouth, or being
hungry, or needing something stronger after an extensive dinner, he or
she might be stressed, tired, have a sensitive stomach etc. There are so
many aspects we have missed before!"*

"How do you collect that kind of information?"

*"A simple test at the entrance to the coffee shop, a small machine you
can choose to interact with, it takes seven seconds."*

*"Sound expensive, but a bit new I must admit, but how does it all
work together?"*

"Let me give you the big picture, everything in our industry nowadays is not really about AI, it is about Customer Experience. If you zoom out you might see self-driving cars, industry robots and AI-spaceships, but now we, companies working with technology, are just trying to help companies to take care of customers better than we used to do. And AI could be a great tool, and provide a competitive advantage. But the basics need to be there, which means, and pay attention now; a lot of relevant and useful data about product facts and then the individual customer profiles. That raises a few questions; how to gather data and what models to use to make something out of it, and how do we apply it as customer service? The reason it's all Artificial Intelligence is that with a software solution the system can learn by its own mistakes, it will correct the behavior over time, just like a human being. We, real people, take in all kinds of information in a given situation, we judge it and then act. Then with the outcome we learn how to adapt to similar situations in the future. An AI-system does the same. And for us, my company, the only thing we are doing is to provide the perfect cup of coffee at each moment for a specific individual customer and we collect data and learn from coffee shops all over the world. So, how's your understanding of coffee and AI now, Mr. Anderson?"

"I might not be totally sold on your coffee service yet, but for sure I have learned more about the big picture of AI, it makes sense to me. I liked the customer experience angle of it, some of my colleagues would love that. And potentially it might be useful to us too. But it's probably too expensive and we also have another challenge, meaning we are a bit special…"

"Tell me about it." Now the waiter is approaching with the food. "And now comes probably the perfectly personalized fish and meat dishes, don't you think? Or maybe they just surprise us with some new flavors! Discovery and personalization is by the way another feature of our coffee solution…Okay, sorry, Mr. Anderson, now you do the talking, tell me how you are special, please, and I'll let you know more about discovery and personalization after that."

Case 2 – a Content Marketing video:

A marketing agency company, Larmate (a fictive company), wants to attract new customers to their content marketing services and they are simply going to post a video on their corporate web and social channels. A few minutes' video and one employee talking. Here is the script:

Hey, marketers.

At first, this was supposed to be a commercial video about Larmate's content marketing services but then we realized that this is exactly the opposite of what we would recommend to you, once you have become our customer. Instead we thought; teach something, and earn trust, keep it open and after that we can see if we should work together or not. Let's get right at it and take a look at the power of content marketing and I will start by giving you the short version of everything you need to know about this topic in order to start making better decisions.

I assume you are a marketer with all your fingers dipped deep down into various kinds of cookie jars of marketing activities. It could be in marketing programs, campaigns, strategic initiatives, tactics, analytical tools, creatives etc. But, by all means, let me start this with a short recap. I assume you are already engaged in many aspects of content marketing, most organizations are, and then you might remember where this all came from? Well, if we look at the most basic and profound piece of content marketing earlier in history, now we are talking about the late nineteenth century when competition wasn't as fierce as today, some initiatives still came along to close the gap in customer relations and the customer magazine was born. A magazine full of content about a specific topic. Obviously, the same topic and context as the actual products they sold. We still see quite a few customer-focused magazines but this can also be compared to what you do on a daily basis as a digital marketer; building customer audiences around blogs and specific topic-driven campaigns with landing pages and content-full websites aligned to the customer journeys. Yes, you know all about that. But it all started much simpler and with the clear goal to own a market, to become the voice of the topic, the place to go to when you had an interest in exactly that topic. Starting to create a long-term relationship with customers, build on trust. Recognize it? Yes, that is because marketing hasn't changed much all over the years in its basic ambition, to design attention, interest and a meeting between a customer and a brand and to eventually lead it to a commercial transaction. It's just that today the playing field is a little bit more complex.

So, we have learned that content marketing comes from a world of creating long term relationships build on trust and nowadays we see a lot of content that is used to quickly attract customers' interest and make them sign up and give out an email address or a phone number, because then you can contact them and the lead gets qualified and down the pipeline you might even convince the prospect to buy something. It is many times acquisition driven and a combination of hard-core sales and a desire for long-term relationship building. But there are exceptions; great ones and also, there is like a movement within content marketing that is working hard to make sure content marketing is used in its best and most respectful and effective ways. To have a content marketing strategy in place, not as much focused on campaigns as before because then you are back to more acquisition focus than long-term relationship building, but think eighteen months ahead, and with patience build your audience, people who actually follow you because they want to, not just because they have to. And that audience becomes your target for quality content marketing over time. And an audience you treat with the fine gloves, with respect and ensure you provide them with targeted value over time, because all the numbers show us that from that audience most business tends to come. That is also why content marketing becomes so attractive. It gives you transactional business and works long term. So basically; pick your areas of expertise, have the ambition to become the expert in your area of the topic, outline a content marketing strategy that bring life to this job, define the audience and start acting with quality and patience. There are tons of other aspects to modern content marketing of course, I just wanted to remind you where we come from and that these are exciting times now because the world of content marketing is changing everyday with new channels and new ways of creating content that is attractive and valuable. Thanks for joining me in this topic today! And let me know about you interest in How to make this all happen for you.

CHAPTER ONE: The Mysterious Customer

THE INDIVIDUAL, THE DISTANCE AND THE MARKETING DESIRE

If you ask me, the most interesting and fascinating aspect of Customer eXperience (CX), Marketing, Sales, Communication, Artificial Intelligence and Teaching is the individual person, the human being, on the other end of the line; the receiver, the customer, the student. That's what makes this as challenging as it is, the complicated human nature, that is why those professions mentioned above becomes hard to figure out. Humans are not typically binary, on the contrary, we often behave inconsistently, illogically and unexpectedly.

As already stated; I argue that we never ever in the history of mankind have experienced this level of education among people in the world, and never ever has the individual person been as insightful and had this kind of access to knowledge, data and information. And we read about numbers like ninety percent of all data in the world has been produced in the last two years, and that data production is probably getting faster and faster. If we put that into the perspective of companies, business models and the way people work, many things come to mind. Additionally, in 1995 only 1% of the global population had access to the Internet, it was one billion in 2005, two billion in 2010, three billion in 2014 and it keeps increasing, soon to probably become half the global population and more. Five hundred years ago there was only about five hundred million people on the whole earth (!) in total, now there are approximately seven billion. Technology has developed at a rapid pace and machines are connected and calculations and estimates indicate that there will be at least 50 billion connected devices in the year 2020: the Internet of Things, IoT. Not to mention the swift development and implementation of Machine Learning, Deep Learning and Artificial Intelligence (AI). No matter whether the numbers are exact or not, the trends are clear and the future is coming, in a philosophical contradictory way, faster towards us, at least when you consider the future as a changed condition.

The context and the world is a complex ball of thread to unravel and understand for each and every individual person. Constantly new prerequisites and conditions we need to relate to. The whole premise of why this is a great time for The Cassiopeia Method is this insightful person with no time and surrounded by a lot of complexity. It is a person who lacks time and mental bandwidth to engage him or herself in every topic of life that needs engagement. In this changed state, and with no signs of this swift development stopping or slowing down, we need new ways to adapt, but in this context Sales, Marketing, Consultancy and Customer Services could add uniquely great value in ensuring this person is met at the right level and helped out. And we should not expect the continuous acceptance of the old practices including manipulation, luring disturbing and mass communication, they would hopefully not be the best practice and as successful in the future. This new customer, student and person appreciates other aspects of companies, the value-driven parts, and the individual person has the power now, for sure.

Digitization. The digital transformation. The world is not just water, earth, wind and fire anymore – it is also a big bubble of data. The world is actually boiling over with data bits forming parts of information that eventually becomes knowledge for us human beings and extra smart computers. This digital transformation has been ongoing since years back, but not with the intensity of today, it is on its way into the future and brings with it huge changes in most aspects of our lives. New technological tools create new behaviors, habits and opportunities. Not to mention what comes with the impressive development within Artificial Intelligence (AI). But does it come naturally to us to want to change? No, not really. Rather to survive. Many people need someone to hold their hand, although not many want to acknowledge that. Also, it can be convenient to keep living in a misty land of not really knowing what is going on, not really understanding or caring about it at all. *Just tell me what I need to know. Otherwise let me be and let me live my life here and now, just give me a cup of coffee and an ordinary printed book on real paper.*

No matter how we consider this or how we feel about it: the world keeps moving. And; *there is only one way to go, and that is to keep moving forward.* Sub cultures will still exist, thoughts and feelings, even for me, where I want to stop time or even turn it back. To a historical situation where things seemed to be better, or at least easier. A way of dressing, attitudes, how music sounded and living the life that seemed to be far more attractive than what we experience here and now. A flight away from the continuous move forward into the unknown. It can be hard. Why can't an ordinary human being just be able to stop and do what he or she does best? Why do you need to be exposed to new demands and requirements every day, expected to understand and adapt to a changing and new world? Many people, I would argue, embrace this constant change with curiosity and acceptance, *it is what it is,* and the personal renewal should be exciting and fresh. And others are quietly saying; *Just give me some support, just tell me what options there are, what they stand for and how other similar persons made their decisions. Just explain to me. In a way that I understand. Make me understand.*

Time and the mental bandwidth have set boundaries in many people's lives. It's really hard to keep up, find the time for it, know what happens here and there, not to mention how to respond to it all. However, at the same time, people have never been as skilled and equipped with such sophisticated awareness. Ever. Thus, if they should listen to anyone, it needs to be someone they have trust in. Someone they might look up to. Someone who can guide them, in a humble and intelligent way, someone that can present the case, in a short executive summary format. That makes it easy to make a decision and act on it. How to do that is obviously what this book is all about because this is a great opportunity for all companies that need to sell their products and solutions, that feel urged to increase the customer face-time of their Sales, Marketing, Consultants and Customer Services in order to create demand and new sales but always need to fight for the customer's attention. This is an opportunity to create trust and a long-term relationship by helping the customers already early on in the phase of Marketing and Sales, not only later when the real product or solution is delivered. This is a way of providing value to customers, instantly and at the same time being relevant, at all stages and at all touch points with customers. To offer a new kind of *customer dialogue.*

This is a true win-win situation.

THE MYSTERIOUS CUSTOMER AND THE VIOLET BUTTERFLY

I call the hard-to-get customer the *mysterious customer.*

The reason is that the new and potential customer is often regarded as mysterious from the other side, from the supplier's point of view. The mysterious customer is one or many people that you often don't really know, or even less know how they think, or feel. There's a distance. On the supplier's side, you can speculate endlessly and discuss whether a customer will act in one or another way. The customer appears to be a shadow, a movement in the twilight, someone you sometimes confuse with an illusion, an imagination, a hope. And since the customer many times provides proof of the distance and tends to build a high wall surrounding themselves in order to protect themselves from aggressive Sales and Marketing actions, the supplier's side soon starts to fantasize and speculate around who that customer really is, what he or she wants and needs. You start making assumptions, applying logic, argumentation and guesswork. A group of Sales representatives could soon totally agree on a solid business case for a specific customer, they hardly met, a business case impossible to reject considering the self-explaining impressive return on investment coming from buying the product. Marketers tend to even less often, or never, meet and talk to real and physical customers, so what they do is to listen to *the truth* from the Sales representatives, or the Consultants, read analyst reports and conduct surveys, and it often ends up with half-baked stories.

What keys could you use instead? How could you open up the doors to the mysterious customers? Or even better, how do you make customers open up the doors themselves and welcome you in? Well, simply by helping them without being a threat. Or disturbance. Sales and Marketing have known for many years that they need to be a solution to the customer's problem but they most of the time don't execute on that because they are occupied with the mission to make the customer become interested, attracted and to buy something. No matter what. And in many cases, they have a hard time knowing what else to do, it sounds so good to help the customer, and I believe most people within Sales and Marketing would love to do that, be of help, but they simply don't know what to do every time. Because they are not consultants or part of the delivery team, they don't always know enough to advise the customer by providing details. Here is an area where I would argue that there are other and better ways to proceed, and that would be by educating the customer, not only educating how the product works, but how different parts of the market category works, sharing best practice, putting the specific customer situation into the big picture and starting to zoom in and out etc. Obviously, customers today appreciate learning more about the contexts and many different aspects of the topic. But it is important that it is *education* and not just Sales and Marketing in an education disguise.

Another story.

A violet butterfly is a beautiful image from nature, a small and colorful butterfly. You know a fantastic creation you suddenly might see and experience in the summer time. The butterfly just appears, you weren't prepared, but now you just want to follow its flight, see where it's heading, hopefully see it take a break, land and you get the opportunity to fully embrace the details of this masterpiece in front of your eyes. And you see it land on your stone wall just outside your house, you take a few steps to approach it and sit down just beside it.

This one just happens to be a violet-colored butterfly, it could be other colors, but you somehow understand that this specific color doesn't stand for hostility or send you a signal of *back off!*

No, it is the opposite, the violet butterfly appears to basically want to be seen and appreciated for what it is: a beautiful butterfly. Then it strikes you, the butterfly is always quiet, no sounds, and it seems to be impossible to predict its movements, it seems to be shy or at least always creating a feeling of distance, or not really be able to see you, care about you. This violet butterfly is just doing its thing, it just is, in its own world, occasionally passing you during a flight, probably on its way to the next flower. Then somehow you realize from somewhere back in your mind that you have at some point in time learned that butterflies remind you of the sad story of how short a life could be. A day? And you realize that no one's life is particular long and this creates a need within you to act, to approach the butterfly, to get to learn to know it, to engage, before it is too late.

Hey, little friend, how can I help you? You reach out your hand, hoping to see a reaction, but you don't even really know if the butterfly has eyes, at least you can't see any on this violet one on the stone wall, you don't know much about butterflies, do you? But one thing you do know, and you then slowly take back your outreached hand, you can't touch the butterfly, because you would probably crush it, or hurt it.

The violet butterfly is a delicate reminder, that you now can't be with, or without. You realize a couple of things. Firstly, you can't catch and control everything and expect it to be as you thought it would be, you need to accept that some things come and go and to enjoy it while it last, like this short moment with the butterfly. Secondly, the violet butterfly could be compared to human beings in this world, with the distance, shyness, complexity and behind a door that seem to be closed. Still, many times beautiful butterflies and unique individuals, are not typically against you, they are just restricted and have their own agenda and flight routes.

Many times, this picture helps me to understand people around me, at least to respect them even more, and to see and consider customers in their everyday life. To look at customers before you have created a relationship with them as violet butterflies, it might help you too, they could be truly mysterious and complicated to predict, and you want to be with them, not only because you have something to sell, but because they interest you, they fascinate you. The image of the violet butterfly reminds me to be humble towards whomever I communicate with in this business of Marketing and Sales. I communicate with this mysterious butterfly with respect and accept the initial distance and that I have to learn that some butterflies just fly away and you'll never see them again and some of them actually stay with you on the stone wall for a while. And you learn to just appreciate this.

For me, everything in the earlier stages of Marketing and Sales is centered around this violet, mysterious butterfly, super hard to attract and create a relation with. It's more fascinating and interesting and value-driven than other more transactional aspects of business that come as natural stages and outcomes when you learn how to approach the butterfly with the right style and mindset.

The violet butterfly is the mysterious customer – and the quest of our profession!

And this awareness and respect eventually becomes one of the cornerstones of The Cassiopeia Method. To *see* the customer in the moment.

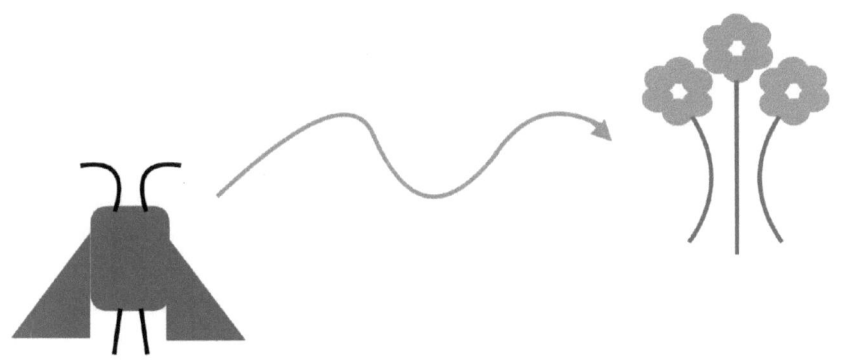

Picture 1. The violet butterfly is the mysterious customer.

HEAR THE SONG OF THE CUSTOMER

We have heard the song a few years now.

The song of the Customer.

Or the age of the Customer. And it feels like it will never go away again.

It's a beautiful song and it's a favorite one. Because it is right, it is service minded, it is mature and grown up. It's not that we haven't understood the importance of the customer before, we always knew that. And talked about it politely and correctly. The importance. It was just that it wasn't hundred percent needed, since the competition wasn't that tough as we experience it now. We still hear the slogans; *put the customer in the center* or *it's important with customer value* or *we need to be customer focused*. But many times, it stays with talk, pep talk and an assumed approach. And we still see organizations with the inside-out execution and prepared to do anything to win customers and business, sometimes forgetting to do anything for their customers.

It's natural, it takes time to change, and the reason to change must be even clearer. It is highly likely that we'll see a significant change in the future. More companies with *true* customer service in mind. Because they have to change. They have to become customer obsessed, we have heard that too, and more and more companies actually embrace that approach and do what they can to implement it in their culture, execution and strategy.

It is not enough to just know some parts of the customer's business and what is going on around behavior and needs, personas and trends. To be customer obsessed you need to engage in the extreme, even know the customer's business better than the customer does.

And this should not be misunderstood and confused and be interpreted as the customer decides everything. Well, in some sense they will decide everything but it doesn't mean per se that they should be considered to be right all the time. And many customers appreciate vendors that argue with them, challenge them. As Steve Jobs once said:

"A lot of times people don't know what they want until you show it to them."

Nevertheless, the song of the customer is sometimes the song *by* the customer. I like the thought of a song *for* the customer. A song they are open to and willing to listen to. And in the best of cases, continuing the metaphor, the customer sings *with* you, like a duet where I lead but in tune with the customer. An alignment of skills, courage and interest – exploring new ways and dimensions together.

This is the ambition of The Cassiopeia Method, described in detail later in the book.

PERSONALIZATION – ONE UNIVERSE FOR EACH CUSTOMER

Once upon a time there were kings and queens ruling the world, and once upon a time there were clergymen saying what was right or wrong, once upon a time there were economists trying to come up with answers and nowadays there are engineers setting the agenda with ever new technology. But soon we will be as educated and refined as we can be and will be longing for warm empathetic and humanistic philosophers, they will be the ones we will listen to. My prediction. Or wish.

After all, we are all humans. Little has changed during our time, yet incredibly much.

With all due respect to the long list of influencers, the latest authority with lots of power is: the customer.

And especially the customer as a human being.

Let us stay for a while with this *human being*. A creature with the complexity of being a unique individual with its own universe, mysteries and secrets. Just the fact that not everything about an individual personality and behavior is pure logic and rational creates this quality of being unpredictable. At the same time, there is always the other side of the coin and that is the construction of the human being, the needs and instincts that are basic for the animal nature and therefore easy to identify, understand and foresee. A man needs water and food to survive, a reasonable temperature and opportunities of procreation. Maslow's hierarchy of needs is classic and is often built up as a pyramid with parts: Physiological, Safety, Love/Belonging, Esteem and Self-Actualization. This model has been around for a while and there are debates as to whether it is still relevant or correct but in this context, it serves perfectly to describe how a human being basically works. To fully understand this model, it is helpful if you work with a customer and try to really understand how various reactions and behaviors arise from deeply rooted biological qualities and prerequisites. In many parts of the world, people have come far up in the hierarchy of needs and you preferably need to satisfy their desire of appreciation and opportunities to Self-Actualization rather than more basic psychological needs. Aligned to that, many corporate brands work in quite an advanced way with the ambition to meet customers at the highest levels of the model, to position the brand in the right context and help customers with appropriate activities.

But I am not bringing up our basic human needs and higher ambitions here to discuss branding, it's rather about seeing who we really are – still, even in a changed world. When the wheels are turning fast and new technology is replaced with even newer technology, the society and people need to adapt. We experienced it many times through new capabilities like the Internet, Social Media and Mobility – the whole information and data explosion. And Artificial Intelligence (AI). Despite all those new tools and the fact that we live more in real-time, mobile and can stay in touch with the whole world all the time there are still those basic human needs. Yes, we are moving up the hierarchy of needs but only too often we tend to fall back to the basics, not feeling perfectly calm or safe when we experience challenges around keeping up in the high-speed development and changing world. And that could also affect and confuse our self-esteem and ability to achieve Self-Actualization, not least because when you focus on basic needs your field of vision narrows down and it's harder to see the wider perspective, the strategy, the vision, where you are heading and what you are moving towards. All this is crucial to bring into a world of personalization, which implies customization down to the individual person. That is a practice that has become a reality through scalable and intelligent technology but in the basic version it's all about knowing, respecting and interacting with that unique human being. In a customer context, it is not only about being customer centric, it is much more; it is ultimately interest and empathy for a fellow human being. And it needs to be good and honest, since a human being is equipped with sophisticated warning systems and can recognize manipulation attempts immediately.

THE TONES BEHIND THE CHORDS

Since we have already concluded that the customer is a human being, we should extend this to describe the customer in yet another way, namely as a human being with two significant and important constituent parts.

Rational and *emotional* impact in the context of decision making.

There are many reasons why it is incredibly useful to be aware of this when interacting with people.

Initially we can address the concept of the left and right halves of the brain. The left half of the brain typically stands for words, numbers, logic, analysis, structure and step-by-step thinking. And the right part of the brain stands for imagination, colors, form, the now, intuition and thinking of many things at the same time. We instinctively want to believe that most decision making is done by the left part of the brain but researchers have increasingly argued that it might not be that simple and that *gut feeling* might have a greater impact on decisions than we previously thought.

In a world in which the customer is truly in the center of the business universe it is helpful to be reminded of this, since the rational and hard-core arguments are not automatically and at all times the most important focus when communicating with a customer. All the way back to the 17th century we have been living in an over-dimensioned view of rationalism as the ruling factor. Historically and philosophically, this was in many ways driven by the school of the famous philosopher René Descartes (1596-1650) and embraced by Baruch Spinoza (1632-1677) and Gottfried Wilhelm von Leibniz (1646-1716). Eventually other aspects were considered through the philosophical direction of phenomenology, driven by Edmund Husserl (1859-1938) and inspired rational thinkers like Jean-Paul Sartre (1905-1980).

Today there are arguments proposing that the rational parts are only the ratifications or provide the rational reasons for a decision, and that the decision is actually founded in emotions. Most probably, a combination. At least, that is my gut feeling.

In the brain, we also find the strong reward system driving human behavior decisively to wanting to do certain activities in order to, in the end, receive a reward, a dopamine kick. There are many use cases where this system is misused and drives illness because being unbalanced addicted to certain behaviors. This is well known in the commercial industries, especially the Retail sectors where you want to provide the dopamine-kick integrated into the buying process. In aspects of teaching and education this could be used in order ensure the student receives rewards and energy during the learning journey (and curve). It could be as easy as just to confirming that the student has understood the topic well, or just acknowledging the student by seeing and respecting the student's situation.

The point is, by being interested in the human being, the brain, the driving forces and behaviors, you can adapt and become a better teacher, sales rep, consultant or marketing manager. Become interested in the tones behind the chords when interacting with real people.

CHAPTER TWO: The Hymn of the Customer-Facing Professional

THE CONTEXT OF TEACHING AS A VALUE DRIVER IN A CUSTOMER DIALOGUE

It's a pleasure and honor but not always that easy to face customers.

At least, it is not getting any easier because of all the good reasons already outlined in this book. The customer is now equipped with both high demands and useful weapons to choose whatever way they want. And you can often sense that attitude already in the meeting room, even before you've sold or marketed anything, or given consultancy advice, or even opened your mouth.

The customer wants to be in charge.

Although that doesn't mean they aren't extremely interested in possibly using your services and products. In fact, most customers are looking for a few good suggestions so they can solve their problems. Nothing new about that. Still, there is something about patience nowadays. And part of the reason too, is not only the customer power, it is also the fact that globalization and how we have made so much of all complexities of manufacturing so much easier, accessible and affordable that has driven an explosion in the number of companies in each industry and sector. This is driving enormous contacting activity. All those millions of companies want to sell something and they are doing everything they can to reach out and start a conversation and relationship with all potential customers. This has made the situation for some exposed roles within a company unbearable. Five, ten, fifty calls before lunch, sales reps from all over the world reaching out. And the email inbox is filled with marketing newsletters and the websites full of target advertising through re-targeting, Account-Based-Marketing and advertorial articles. We need to understand and respect that customers typically can't give time, attention and action to everyone and everything. This is when Content

Marketing made an entrance, and Inbound Marketing. Providing value and interacting with the customer only when they seem to be interested and mature enough, through Marketing Automation.

Obviously, in this book, I won't be judging all kinds of vendor activities, I truly recommend learning how to *educate* while having a customer meeting, or while providing a marketing campaign or while providing consultancy advisory or talking to a customer in Customer Support. That recommendation is based on this very tangible need on the part of the customer. To provide the customer-facing professional with the value-driver tools, how to provide the customer with value instantly, by educating them in what is complicated and hard to understand. And there is quite a lot in the world that a customer doesn't have time or mental bandwidth to take in.

In this context there are a few terms describing and defining similar things or at least the terms are connected. *Commercial Teaching* and *Education-Based Marketing* are two terms I like to use because they describe two approaches although they are so broad they could mean many things. Here's what I would encompass in those terms.

- In general, every company has an area of expertise in the market place and this is about how to teach that topic to their market audience. It is teaching with a long-term commercial intent.
- In general, teaching in a brand's context instead of "only" providing traditional Sales pitching and Marketing interruption.
- In general, teaching as in directly helping and providing value to the customer, and indirectly communicating the existence of a brand as a potential supplier of the forthcoming need for solutions.
- In general, teaching and communication in a modern format; short and effective, empathic, aligned to the individual human being and the common hectic agenda.
- By *Commercial Teaching* I mean concrete skills for *customer-facing persons* like Sales, Consultants, Subject-Matter-Experts (SMEs) and Customer Support/Service. Typically used in one-on-one meetings with customers.

- *Education-Based Marketing* is applied by *the Marketing department* for various types of content creation, event presentations and promotion of SMEs. Commercial teaching at scale, but still aligned to individual customer individuals or groups.
- The Cassiopeia Method could be *applied* for both Commercial Teaching and Education-Based-Marketing.

To educate the customer through Sales and Marketing is not new per se, absolutely not, but the potential to have more of it in this fast spinning and increasingly complex world is a huge.

I also suggest that there is an enormous potential for improvement when it comes to the educational aspects; *how* to teach and really make sure the modern man understands and hopefully wants to act and buy. The customer's situation nowadays has changed so much and the need for simple and effective explanations is greater than ever.

But this is not only for the Sales or Marketing departments, this is a solid value-driven way of communicating with customers from most *customer-facing* positions within a company, including consultants, customer service and actually most of the people with a communication touchpoint to customers. In their own context and role.

Another use case.

About a company within the Technology industry with fairly complex products to offer, like software solutions with applications, add-ons and services. I have personally been in that industry for twenty years. The old marketing model would structure a campaign with certain tactics including some advertisement, promotions, events etc. Everything communicated with the right words for that industry, marketing buzzwords and a lot of constructive arguments. Or if you have a more modern version of operations you might align this to a content marketing strategy and produce a lot of content around the products; customer cases, value propositions etc. Publish it on corporate blogs, podcasts, social media etc.

Still, many times, one part is missing; does the customer really *understand* what the offering is actually about, do they understand how it would be great for them and how it truly works?

I would suggest that on many occasions the case is quite the opposite, and the customer would honestly appreciate a shorter communication version with more simple explanations. Preferably aligned to *their* unique situation, somewhat personalized.

During the past couple of years in the era of digital and social media we have seen a huge increase in instructional videos available only a few clicks away. That is great, and we probably will see more of it, but there is also an opportunity for companies to embrace this even further and integrate Education-Based Marketing best practice into the whole customer communication model. To become the Teacher the customer turns to, listens to and trusts. Becomes the number one place to go to and understand and receive an immediate value. The probability that the customer *wants* to buy from the company thus increases, not least due to the concept of reciprocity. Since they get something they feel that they have to pay for it too. They want to give something back to you, could be a *thank* you, but could also mean they want to buy something from you. That often happens when you provide them with, not just an ordinary white paper instruction, as a bad example. This is about customer success, satisfaction and loyalty. This is about Customer Experience. This is a core touchpoint where you can exert a massive influence on the Customer Experience, especially if you are in industries that are complex to grasp and understand.

This is more than just another marketing tactic or activity; this is a potential way of *practice leadership* where the customers and prospects are your followers. And you are the Authority, the leader and the teacher's voice. That means that Education-Based Marketing and Commercial Teaching in parallel will also build a Customer Audience. An audience consisting of your prospects and existing customers, these are the students that you primarily help and not only interrupt with common marketing and sales practice. The way you can see and understand the individual customer is the key to success here, you will see.

It is the key to a phenomenal Customer Experience.

THE RELEVANCE OF CHALLENGE FOR CUSTOMER-FACING PROFESSIONALS

From a customer's point of view, I can easily use my own experience to do that and probably you too; there is very limited patience with Sales, Marketing and Service. Honestly, I am most of the time quite disappointed since too often I leave a conversation with the feeling that the person I talked to didn't really understand my situation, didn't really care or more or less showed openly that his or her objectives were the only ones of importance. Although most of them use sweet talk.

A customer typically just wants the best and most affordable possible help.

Issues connected to solutions.

When we are on the solution side of the equation; and the vendors and suppliers can't meet the customers with the right approach and medicine, the disconnection gap will increase and this is a huge reason why many Sales reps and Consultants have a hard time even getting air-time with a customer. Because what they are saying is not relevant. *The customer doesn't get back to me, doesn't respond to my calls or emails. They are probably very busy, but it is disrespectful!* Well, the truth in many cases is that as long as you are not providing relevance to a customer they will respond conservatively or not at all.

There are many ways you can fix this. I won't simplify this too much, because a lot of aspects relate to this; your brand, your product position, you as a person, the customer's openness and interest in your specific topic at that moment etc.

But there are ways you can increase the probability of becoming relevant over and over again. And that is to constantly be passionately interested in the customer's situation. But that doesn't automatically make that customer want you to come back a second time. You also need to provide value during the meetings. Many of us have read the fantastic book *The Challenger Sale* (Portfolio/Penquin 2011) by Matthew Dixon and Brent Adamson on how you challenge the customer with new aspects of potential solutions and how that might differentiate you from the competition. And you can move even further and be exceptionally good at explaining complex parts of the topic. Educate the customer while in the meeting, bring the customer on a Story Journey. An exercise in the customer conversation, how to instantly be relevant and provide value. To make the discussion even more interesting for the customer and you. If nothing more, the customer gets a higher level of understanding and a good impression of you as a vendor (from the meeting).

It's all about becoming even more relevant as a customer-facing professional.

YOU ARE SELLING – ENLIGHTENMENT BEFORE CHANGE

We know it instinctively.

All we are selling is CHANGE.

Think about it, there is always something that is about to be changed after the purchase. The same when you are buying something without a financial transaction, like an idea. State of mind or the physical condition changes, it will not be same as before you bought something. Yes, it is a bit of a conceptual way of looking at it, but you can learn something from this. *Change* could be dramatic for us and some changes need enlightenment before happening. Change can cause increased stress and concerns. Is this really the right way for me to go? Am I ready? Is it worth it? Do I know what I am doing?

This is where teaching and guidance could be very much appreciated and useful. To take care of the worried person in front of you. Why is this working? Because many times being concerned and worried is part of our internal risk assessment system, it's automatically on, by default. And it doesn't always make sense and those situations could be managed by just talking about it. To unveil the unknown and frightening risks. By providing the larger picture and inviting the person into a state of enlightenment often helps considerably. And then, when the person arrives at that stage and moves on with a decision to buy or not buy, and you have done your teaching job well, trust is earned and you have laid the foundations for a valuable relationship.

A CRYSTAL-CLEAR MARKETING STORY

An embarrassing number of companies and their products are very hard for people to understand, you just don't get their pitch, what they really do and especially how they can help you. In the long run, you might not really care because you don't understand it.

On the other hand, the companies themselves tend to believe that what they do is the clearest thing in the world, because that's what they do every day and they just don't understand how others don't get it.

But didn't we say that modern people and customers are smarter and more educated than ever? Yes, and probably true, but I also argue a couple of times in this book that they are more occupied and limited in time and especially in mental bandwidth on account of everything that goes on in their individual lives. That said, what company would you choose to listen more to, the one that you immediately understand or the one that is still a blur after you have got some kind of communication from them? And I agree the answer is not as simple as to say that everyone choses the company they understand, because nowadays, how do you check what company or product to buy if you don't understand or don't have the time to engage? A popular option is to check for referrals, look at reviews, recommendations, ask colleagues, friends, your industry network. But you would most of the time prefer to understand and be confident, based on your own knowledge and confidence.

Companies with more extraordinary needs for crystal-clear marketing stories are companies within complex industries like the exploding Technology Industry which includes a vast Startup community, and more traditional industries like Banking, Finance, Insurance, Telecom and Utilities. Most of them need to educate the market about their sophisticated solutions to specific problems.

I still face this challenge daily with technology as the big topic; to fit the bits together and understand the technology landscape and map the solutions that are offered and the gigantic wave of new companies that pop up every week and every month. It's fantastic, but it's also crystal clear that companies have to be great at communication with a combination of educating the market about the market category and at the same time pitching why they as a company are unique and stand out. And there we see the combination of commercial and non-commercial. Companies just don't educate the market for free, then they could be a government institution. There are commercial reasons for everything.

A great example, in most Startup contexts it is crucial to be the first company to attract early adopters and build an audience. It is essential to establish the first relationship with customers before all the potentially upcoming competition wakens up. The customers are more likely to stay with their existing vendor rather then switch over later if they don't have strong reasons for doing so. There is apparently much to be gained from quickly and effectively coming out and transforming the customer's mind. From not knowing anything about a solution to the problem, a problem they might not have be thinking of, to understanding, enlightening and eventually becoming more mature be able to take the next steps. Subsequently, that would ideally lead to the customer starting to buy and lead to an ongoing healthy and valuable relationship.

A crystal-clear marketing story should not only be about pitching a cool marketing campaign or simply building a brand. Everyone can do that with creative agencies and big marketing budgets. On the other hand, the marketing approach should not be filled with all kinds of clutter content; marketing solutions that don't make the customer clearer on what is actually being offered. No, keep the focus and tell a story that starts with the individual customer's situation and context, assume they don't understand as much as you think, respect their limited time and mental bandwidth and tell them in a brief and simple format what your thing is about, in what context you operate, what the solution is and how simply it can become a part of the everyday life of the individual customer. Telling something in a pedagogical way requires skill and it is not necessary the same thing as presenting a nice sales pitch.

When you have communicated with the customer they should be able to say:

Thanks! I do really get it, I pretty much see what your products could do for me, I also just learned some new things I have been thinking of and wonder about, you are one of the few around who can teach and make ordinary people understand, and since you also seem to be a source of valuable help I will follow you to start with.

Picture 2. A crystal-clear marketing story.

CONTENT MARKETING STRATEGY

Content Marketing is the umbrella; it is where you typically place the initiatives for broader usage of The Cassiopeia Method, applied specifically. Those initiatives could have many names; Education-Based Marketing, Commercial Teaching, Training, Subject-Matter-Expert programs, blogging etc. But it should not stay within the Marketing sphere, it has enormous potential in other or all point of interactions with customers. Imagine when a customer is calling a customer support and gets to talk to someone who not only solves the problem but is also able to hear and understand where the customer is. And is able to explain fast (and entertainingly) how the context works in order to make sure the individual understands enough to be able act on it independently, as well as also deepening the trust and ensuring a healthy relationship. There you have the ROI, Return-On-Investment, for using the Cassiopeia Method, together with increased Customer Satisfaction ratings.

Content Marketing has, with help from all new technology, exploded and has become best practice for companies to tell stories and offer all kinds of valuable and entertaining content, in an ambition to build value-driven relationships, loyalty and audiences. Content Marketing is looked upon as a more cost-effective and focused way of marketing compared with traditional advertising. And within the realm of Content Marketing the notion of Education-Based Marketing content is far from new, in fact it is many times central to the initiatives. The challenge is that this is often done as a training course or as a softer version of a sales pitch. Most times you miss a true pedagogic approach, there is huge potential to lift most Content Marketing initiatives that have educational aspirations, to reach new levels of appreciation when they become truly understandable for the individual customer.

What do I mean by *pedagogic*?

It is basically about ensuring that your students really understand your lessons, *really understand*, and it is just as simple as that.

Many teachers, marketers and key note speakers think and believe they provide clear and understandable teaching and that their audience really gets it, but often the audience doesn't get it and won't admit it. They aren't always honest about it because of the basic human behavior that you don't want to appear as trivial or uneducated, people just don't want to admit they don't get it, or they might not want to hurt the feelings of the presenter. Eventually, we end up with applause and standing ovations to key note speakers while the audience leaves the room with the sinking feeling that they probably just heard something important, but honestly, they still have problems understanding and figuring out how to apply it in their everyday situations.

And this has become one of the biggest challenges for Content Marketing, it is just a lot of content, and not packaged to fall into the right places inside the head of the individual student or customer. And this is not easy, as in most professional approaches it takes talent, tools and hard work. And in this book, coming up, we focus on tools, techniques and methods for how to become more pedagogical and become a modern teacher, updated and equipped for today's stressed human being, the student and customer.

THE POWER OF GREAT TEACHING

Teaching nowadays is practiced in many contexts and with ever-changing groups of students.

Basically, there used to be one main public school for everyone and one authoritative teacher telling you what things you need to learn, what things you needed to memorize and what proven methods to learn in order to solve standard problems. Why and how.

When you talk to individuals about their attendance at school in younger years they tend to remember their childhood in terms of exactly what teachers they appreciated and considered as great teachers (and also with clarity remember the worst ones). Why were the great teachers appreciated as teachers? Common explanations describe aspects of the teacher as; just, distinct, acted with clarity, competent, easy to understand and often the teacher *saw you*.

I would rank teaching as one of the most underestimated professions we have. In relation to how important it is for people and the society.

Teaching that generates true results achieved in the student's mind and as practical and usable abilities, and sometimes with this great feeling as a student to have arrived at next stage or phase on a development curve.

The biggest issue I experience is when students, or customers, don't *really* understand. They just learn enough to survive the moment. Or they honestly don't understand and their solution is to learn the method, memorize and pass the test. There could be various reasons for this behavior but many times the problem is that no one seems to be there with the ability and time to explain the topic for the student in a reasonable and understandable way. It's not always a lazy student's fault, most times it is the inability of a teacher to teach a topic in a comprehensible manner. Because they just present facts and hand out tasks. Or apply some standardized approach, not enough customization. When you start to treat and look upon students as customers and vice versa something happens, you might learn something and change your attitude and approach. Yes, the customer is paying and everything you do is dependent on the customer's response, but you can't blame them for inabilities, you need to figure out how you as a vendor could better meet their needs. And the same goes for students, you can't blame bad results on bad students all the time (I am aware and have experienced that there are situations where no teaching seems to help and instead you need something else, like a high ranking military officer threating with penalties...). Basically, you just need to do the teaching job better.

If you want to achieve remarkable teaching you need to start thinking in other ways. And that starts in the student's mind. *Their* state of mind.

This is the time for remarkable teachers, modern teachers, with all the data floating around and with the ultra-speed changes we experience every week, we truly would appreciate it if someone could step forward and explain, describe and *teach* what is happening. Nicely, calmly and simply, sketch out the patterns, let us see how data points are connected and why. Someone needs to do this with skill, humility, a sense of pedagogy and deliver with some level of entertainment.

A modern teacher and preacher.

Why is it that you rarely experience a truly good teacher in a business context? Or a marketing and sales practice that you actually appreciate? How can companies over and over again choose unappreciated ways to engage with their customers instead of simply helping the customers to understand how things work in the context of the product?

I have provided answers to that and built the case for a new approach.

The truth is that sometimes I as a customer am in the mood for *yes, I want to understand it all*, but other times I simply feel *I don't care about all details or how it really works, just tell me what is best for me*, but in order to follow someone's advice I need to *trust* them. And that trust is easily established for a person who seem to be able to explain how it all works. A teacher's voice.

Great teaching creates trust.

And all commercial actors know that trust is the golden place to be. All kinds of profitable effects come from that, especially customer loyalty.

But is there a magical skill in becoming a great teacher? Why haven't business people made this their number one skill to be good at? Aside from closing business techniques. At least their customer facing professionals. After an infinite number of classes in *presentation skills,* how can it be that very few people seem to be able to calmly explain how things work? And not just to stack up memorized sales arguments and try to make it look like education, that is just selling in disguise. And I as a student or a customer see and hear it, and become tired and unfortunately none the wiser. But I do get kind of used to it.

Personally, since I have been working on teaching and presentation skills for many years now as a teacher, marketer, sales professional, consultant, manager and leader, I frequently get the feedback from satisfied students, customers and colleagues that *they finally understood, thank you very much.*

However, we need to crack the code to being great teachers.

Great teachers in modern versions, delivering explanations in short versions, highly pedagogic, sometimes personalized and in an entertaining manner, build on an updated foundation of knowledge of the topic, from a gigantic ocean of digital and physical information.

A storyteller who summarizes and gives actionable insights.

Enough rambling about the business case, the reasons behind and the overall approach to the challenge, I assume you get the point more than well. The Why and What are fairly obvious now.

Let's look into the How and The Cassiopeia Method.

CHAPTER THREE: The Cassiopeia Method

THE STAR PERSPECTIVE

The Cassiopeia Method is about how to communicate with the empowered customer, an individual under pressure of time and limited mental bandwidth, using a teaching style that is appreciated. This is one way and my primary suggestion on HOW to approach *Refreshing The Customer Dialogue.*

It's conversational in the sense of an authority teaching with complete alignment to the customer and student.

It's an optimal way of adding value while having a conversation face to face with the customer. One-on-one or one-to-many. You provide a new level of *understanding.*

And *The Cassiopeia Method* is the name of it and for many good reasons.

Obviously, Cassiopeia is a known star constellation in the Northern Hemisphere, and not only do I personally originate from the North but more important is the symbol value of the appearance of this star constellation. Since it circulates around the Northern star Polaris it's appearance varies during the seasons. Primarily, I appreciate it when it looks like the letter "W", because it's the perfect picture of The Story Journey, like a process map with steps that are one big part of The Cassiopeia Method. Then the constellation also looks like the number "3" and that is corresponds with the parts The Cassiopeia Method consists of; The Content Basis, The Look and The Story Journey. And then as an extra bonus the star constellation sometimes looks like the letter "M", as in my first name. And this might be the only time I am being a bit self-centric in this context, otherwise the most important point of the whole method is an extreme focus on the customer, the student, the situation, and how to constantly align in the moment through cognition and an individually customized didactic application, pedagogy, curriculum – because that is what is mostly missing in traditional teaching and that is what the modern customer expects and appreciates.

But the fact that Cassiopeia is a star constellation and the name of the method is also connected to the importance of perspectives in teaching. A big part of the teaching and communication technique I provide is about picking the right perspectives, aligned to the universe of the student. And the name Cassiopeia should be the obvious reminder to always consider various perspectives, more often than not a big perspective, a star perspective.

The Cassiopeia Method is built up from three parts, determinately because it should be easy to remember when you encounter a customer meeting or whatever contact you have with someone you want to have a value-driven communication with, in the context of a complex topic that you understand. And since the topic is fairly complicated a solid foundation is needed for this, and that is the content basis, the research, the acquirement of knowledge, and the current status in the area of interest. The Cassiopeia Method is ultimately supposed to build trust and in order to do that you need to leave the superficial fragmented one-minute-web search content world. This means that you need to do solid work to really understand the topic you are supposed to clarify to customers. Basically, you need to know it well enough to be able to explain the topic high-level to an eight-year old child, then you have probably learned the basics well enough.

Then you move to the next step, and that part might be a significant differentiator from all presentation skills and teaching styles we can find out there, you need to understand the student in extreme, you need to see, watch and enhance everything you can find out about the receiver of your communication. Not only by reading the generic marketing persona descriptions or treating a group as a group, but also by creeping inside the mind of the actual person you are talking to, and finding out as much as possible on what is going on mentally and physically. Because this is what mostly determines the starting point of the communication, and the way the journey moves forward.

The journey should be a story journey in clear steps, but it shouldn't only be facts presented in a logical order, every part should make sense in building a mental picture of what you are trying to explain. You are actually painting a picture in the student's mind. That is also one of the key parts of The Cassiopeia Method: to build up a mental picture while holding the student by the hand during the walk through the new landscape with stops for acknowledgement and reflection as well as crystal clear and potentially constant changes in perspectives – you paint the picture and finally receives the smile and student's acknowledgement *I get it!*

How hard could that be?

Well, there are a number of ways you can make this practice work and it all depends on the context. I picture first and foremost the actual customer meeting, to encapsulate this into a natural conversation. To add value while talking to the customer, provide insights and educate, give value and gain trust. As stated, highly appreciated. But it could also be in other formats; whitepaper, video, webpages, in-classroom teaching, keynote, blog, podcast etc.

You need to carefully choose the right tools and the right approach. Coming from a balanced consideration between what communication techniques you are delivering with ease and in what channels the students are receiving.

Over the years, I have developed best practices for the *teaching moment*, how to really make sure that what I teach really resonates and stays with the student. Over ten years in various teaching formats for kids and youths, a fantastic challenge to lead them into a learning mode, make them become open to listening and learning and to use specific tools and techniques to reach all the way into their minds. Then, for fifteen years I have, almost all my time, been in moments of interaction with customers where I've been trying to explain and teach the complexities of software, business and digital transformation. How to connect Customer Experience all the way back down to legacy systems and databases.

Remember, this is about teaching something, making it stick with understanding, but there is also a commercial intent behind it. You are selling something but that just comes with the package, still the teaching/learning is at the center, you never want the customer to feel abused or deceived. Then the whole finesse of this as an appreciated version of Sales and Marketing falls apart.

Instead, *see* the student and tell a crystal-clear marketing story, crystal clear for the customer, not only for you, and make sure they learn something useful. And create a great Customer Experience, in a dialogue format, it's a constant interaction.

FOUNDATION ONE – THE CONTENT BASIS

Since the end game of all this is primarily to create trust you have to do a solid ground job, meaning knowing what you are talking about. People are smart and sensitive in general and can easily sense when somehow you are presenting something at a superficial level, that you are unsecure about the cornerstones of the topic. You better build your house on a mountain, stable for tough and skeptical criticism.

The good thing is that nowadays there are beneficial ways and great tools to get the research done faster and more effectively. The skill of Digital Curation for sure, but also to use specific tools to gather relevant information. Artificial Intelligence is on everyone's lips at the moment and will probably stick around for years with ever improving services coming up. That is and will be an interesting area for a Digital Curator to follow since Big Data has become significant, real and useful. And at the same time almost impossible for a human being to process and go through. So, there needs to be a process in place to *gather* the right information, and not only evergreen information, but also super-fresh and updated information, not to mention the analyses and reflections and insights.

The world is global; it is made up of billions of people and the distance between any two persons is almost zero. Thanks to technology we have got a global world with a global market place, that means it is harder to build your brand on local presence only.

We should expect more and more competition from other specialists and see a huge increase in the number of extreme niche players; people and companies that focus on detailed defined niches and then go global in that micro-industry.

For instance, it's not generally enough to have an overall focus on *bicycles for the family.* By now you need to fine-tune the niche on how to serve every person in the world with the interest and maybe passion for *classic Italian style bicycles for the whole family from the mid nineteenth century* and you should be able to provide all kinds of product details, history, availability and show everyone that it is impossible to find any more passionate and knowledgeable source, offering a reasonable price, and with the ability to deliver the product in an easy way.

If you are a Startup company within technology, then it makes even more sense to go global in a niche since you don't have the same logistic challenges as with physical products.

Basically, lead the niche.

You build an unheard-of knowledge base by conducting daily digital curation, meaning that you continually dig up all kinds of news, updates and the latest around what's happening in your niche. And then you process the information; analyze, consider insights, conclusions, and make suggestions and recommendations and package it all in appropriate channels. Most popular are various types of social channels.

Nevertheless, I argue that it is primarily about building an authoritative voice as a digital curator, building the bases of fresh and updated educational content and secondarily it is about the format or channel. Assign this work and passion to the most suitable person or persons in your organization and let them dive into this world of information and constant flow of new insights to be shared. It's the work for a passionate attitude so be sure to pick an interesting topic!

Everything you learn during this digital curation process is potentially something you can put into your educational content, and when you start doing it well, you offer a respected authoritative teaching voice that the audience will come back to, wanting to hear the latest *being explained*, because here is where you stand out: acting as a Digital Curator and a Teacher.

BUILDING BLOCKS AND RELATIONSHIPS

This is the way I do it. I engage in a topic by structuring it with significant pieces, the most important building blocks of the context. Starting high level, seeing through the clutter and simplify. Basically, have in mind as the first objective that of being able to explain the topic for an eight-year-old child. And when I have identified the most important building blocks I look closer into their relationships, how they relate to each other and try to see the basic drivers making situations change in the context. Then I zoom out and look at the topic from outside and really try to simplify, thinking how dark matter in the universe is understood, then how difficult can this specific topic be? Then I try to explain it out loud, preferable to someone you trust or otherwise just to yourself. Try it, be a teacher, you are now the teacher for a group of eight-year-old children and they have to be able to explain the topic after you have gone through it with significant parts such as; the basic blocks, the relationships, the drivers and the big picture. Then you turn it all around and close in on the topic by structuring around the three interrogatives Why, What and How. It is so easy and so powerful. Especially, when you are able to understand the Why you have really begun to understand the essence of the topic.

- *Content building blocks* – the big obvious parts, simplify and don't pick too many.
- *Relationships* – see how the building blocks are connected and how they affect each other and potentially are related through processes.
- *Context* – how does it all fit together in a world of other close contexts.
- *Zoom out* – look at the topic from above, put yourself on the moon for a couple of seconds.
- *Articulate* – say it out loud, there is enormous power in actually saying it rather than only thinking about it.

Then, when you have done the ground work of the topic, when you have understood and engaged initially in the topic it is time to go through it again, a bit deeper and start to create the basis on which to become an Authority. That is of course not always necessary, it depends on the situation and the ambition, but the modern human being and customer comes with higher demands on topic excellence which leads us to the fundamental recommendation of not cheating on the research job, do it well, knowledge is an easy burden to bear. And it will pay off later in The Cassiopeia Method. The third part, the Story Journey, becomes so much more solid and trustworthy when you master the topic. Now, let's move on and look at how to build an authoritative voice based on solid knowledge.

DIGITAL CURATION AS A SOURCE

A Digital Curator is a fairly new role and arises from a combination of art history and an exploding digital and social web. A classic Curator is not new at all and belongs in the context of a Museum and being responsible for the art treasures, owning the insights of the background, the knowledge of the art, acting as the content expert, basically being the source of information and knowledge about the artwork and the history behind them all. Being the single source of expertise in the area of the collections of art. Covering most or all aspects of knowledge and ownership, a Curator is a person with deep knowledge in the niche. Subsequently, a similar type of character has arisen in the new tech and media savvy world. In times of globalization and real-time it is impossible for every one of us to keep updated, follow and understand every aspect and part of the new high-speed universe of modern man. We need people who cover different areas, niches, people who own their territory, who keep track of everything that happens and are able to *curate* the most important parts and distribute that information to the rest of us. Digital Curators often distribute their concentrated information assets through social media, blogs and email-lists. They have an important role for all of us helping us to keep up without having to be all over the place ourselves.

Digital Curation is about constantly sweeping information sources within the chosen niche, give them some thought and then sharing the most important parts with others. There are different ways to approach it and it has a lot to do with your personal preferences. But somehow a true interest of the topic to begin with helps a lot, you might not normally want to use the word *passion* but this time it could make sense, because the best Digital Curators have an almost unhealthy interest in their niche, they just can't stay away from looking at, listening to and reading about everything there is, and then they love to share it with the world.

That leaves us with the first action: pick a topic you are madly in love with.

Then it is all about a three-step process that starts over and over again.

The first step in this process is to find and gather relevant information, and in order to do that you need to have skills and tools. This is tricky because this skill is constantly changing because of the ever-moving technology landscape, and literally every day new sources of information pop up. I recommend that you search using key words and early on identify other key influencers, news sources, analysts, vendors and forums of discussions, pictures and movies. Find your ten, twenty or thirty sources of updated information and come back and touch base often and consistently, and be open to adding new ones all the time. No matter whether you prefer to read, listen or look, the options are probably out there. Information gathering is the foundation for a Digital Curator.

You could, and this is common practice among Digital Curators, skip step two and move directly to step three and share the unfiltered information immediately. That is fine but if there is to be a Digital Curation practice worth something extra then step two needs to be included.

The second step is when the Digital Curator reflects, analyzes and produces their own a point of view and opinion about certain news, happenings or updates. And that personal angle and way of looking at the specifics is what is mainly shared in the third step. The reflections could be of any kind. There are Digital Curators giving quite strict facts-driven conclusions, and there are others who just reflect in an entertaining sort of way. And then most Digital Curators try to create a point of view that puts them in a knowledge strong position, they intend to become an *authority*. Say things that make people listen to and highly respect you. My recommendation if you want to become a high-profile premium Digital Curator, not just someone who reiterates others' information, you should spend extra time on step two and really come up with great thoughts and truly add something to the niche.

The third step is about getting the message out there, being heard and acknowledged. The challenge here is the huge clutter of information, content and voices out there in social media and on the web. And if you don't want to buy yourself into the game and buy space to be seen you should combine a long-term engagement in the topic, build relationships, and become an institution other people recommend. Be active in the discussion, share your insights generously and make sure you stay close to your own unique voice. The only unique thing left in this world is individual personalities, use that. And become an authority Digital Curator we all want to follow.

Picture 3. Digital Curation.

FOUNDATION TWO – THE LOOK

The Look is a favorite part of The Cassiopeia Method, mostly because this is the key missing part in most other methods or techniques for effective communication and teaching. Of course, there are always sentences and parts that aspire to highlight the importance of understanding the customer and the student, we have persona-descriptions in Sales and Marketing and we have target groups and analyses around customer behavior, needs and desires. But still, too few seem to really understand and accept that all human beings are unique, truly one of a kind and not only that; the moment you communicate with a consumer it might be the first time and never happen again. Ever. It's all unique moments, and still, we often want to categorize and minimize it all into generic customers and generic behaviors, and the reasons for that could be many. One could be that we rationalize as a human being, to survive and to simplify is the only way we can understand the world. That is a great strategy in part one of The Cassiopeia Method; The Content Basis, when we structure a topic. But it is not the same when it comes to human beings due to the uniqueness factor. Another explanation could be that you get lazy and try to become more productive by drawing conclusions based on previous experience, so you look at people's behavior and the moment you recognize the same behavior you simply draw the conclusion that it will all probably repeat itself.

And the moment you start doing that, not treating every person as a unique moment and individual, you have started *a disconnect process*. In the worst case the receiver of the information never really connects with you, there is no real trust because you don't really care about the human being in front of you. And you haven't even recognized this slight change in relationship balance.

THE GAME CHANGER: SEE AND HEAR WHAT THE CUSTOMER _REALLY_ SAYS AND SILENTLY COMMUNICATES

To see and hear what the customer really says and silently communicates is the key to success for the modern teacher and a customer-facing professional.

To know what you are teaching, being an expert on the topic, is just table stakes. To see through the human being you are communicating with, all the way through layers of non-clarity, non-security, anger, power plays etc.

This is the most important skill I personally have and the most important skill I am trying to teach you about, because that is the number one key to unlocking the potential of a customer relationship.

I am actually quite stunned and surprised how little of this you find in popular books and training on presentation skills.

Most of the times when I am presented something, it doesn't matter if it is an audience of one or an audience fifty people I can just conclude that the presenter not only has no idea on what planet my mind is, but the presenter doesn't seem to have been doing any significant research or showed much interest in the individuals they are talking to. The big mistake and misguidance is most of the times that they are approaching a group. I know, because I fall into the bad behavior myself sometimes, because it is easier to just focus on the topic and it is not always so easy to know how to learn more about the individuals you are approaching with your communication.

The basic recommendation on how to get on to this task is to simply unleash your honest interest. Open your eyes; see, watch and look for what is behind the face you are observing. Look into their eyes, try to figure out where the person is in terms of concentration, interest and emotions. Is there fear, anger, courage, ambition. Of course, it is hard to identify the education and maturity level of all persons in a crowd but that is not an excuse for skipping it altogether, you might need to apply some balance to your research when it comes to formal educations, job experiences and so on, you might need to just pick a few. But if the communication takes place with just a few persons, like a Sales meeting, it's very simple to make sure you understand the human being behind the customer by simply asking them a few questions at the beginning of the meeting, their background, their way into this situation and topic. All the things they are not willing to verbally reveal you need to detect with your eyes and intuition.

How do you do that?

Intuition is a well-concealed and forgotten tool in modern business life. Only too often we adapt facts to become proof of what people think and stand for. Although we all know that is not always the truth. Let me give you an example. You are in a selling situation, you thought you made the sell but then suddenly the customer says they have to choose your competitor. You ask why and they refer to a lower price, there is not enough in the budget for your premium price. Tough luck! And you start to negotiate on the price of course, because that's what they said, the price is wrong! But would the customer admit it if there were more sensitive reasons behind the decision? Maybe the reasons are that you and your team are the kind of persons they don't want to work with. Not many customers want to say that out loud, how do you even say a thing like that? Of course, they point at the price and the budget. When you get rejections or objections from customers you are often more effective when you first really try to figure at the real reasons behind them. This is often the case when you never seem to really understand why the customer chose a worse product than you have and they keep talking about the price even if you adjust the price and lower it. There are other reasons behind it, could be one of several, but more often than not probably something personal. And it's exactly in this sphere, in the complex human being and invariably not fully rational behavior that you need to muster all the inner wisdom you might have. To see, listen and feel what is going on in the room, and then align your communication to that. That is the next part of The Cassiopeia Method, how you structure the communication based on what you learn before and even more importantly: what you learn instantly while engaging with the customer and student. The power of true understanding of who you are dealing with could unfold your most successful moments. That is where all great alignment starts, that is the place where you can connect on deeper levels than just facts. And that is the place you want to be in order to create true trust between yourself and the student.

Because you show that you *care*.

Because you show that you see the unique person.

Has someone ever really seen *you*? Seen through you and really cared. Then you know the power in this. But be careful, this is a place where you need to behave appropriately and truly have good and honest intentions, because if you start to manipulate when you have been invited into the next sphere of the customer you could be burned forever.

This is a great place with high stakes.

You might still wonder: how exactly do I learn how to do this?

THIS IS HOW YOU SEE THE STUDENT

This is a significant process step in The Cassiopeia Method and exactly How, When and at What depth depends on the situation. But it's imperative to understand that this needs to be done every time, because this is the game-changer, otherwise you are just the same as every other presenter, teacher or marketing content producer out there. Sometimes I do this properly as a part of preparing a certain meeting or lecture, but maybe most of the times it takes place in my mind just before the speaking gig or meeting and is quite intensive at the beginning of the meeting as part of the early round-table introductions where you can shoot one or two extra questions, just to build up a somewhat clearer picture of the person you are soon to take on an educational journey. Thus, spend some time on research before the meeting, but most important is the research in real-time during the meeting, many vital aspects are instantaneous and can only appear there and then. People are full of emotions, and they vary over time and the capability to assimilate educational content effectively depends on how many of the important mental doors that are open or shut. You need to knock on some of them and get invited into the world of the student, and encourage interest and do it with trust and decisiveness. Here is a list of things you should be looking for in your *always-on-research*;

- *Formal prerequisites*; education, job experience, title, expertise areas etc.
- *Human maturity*; situation in life, what's going on holistically 24*7.
- *Position in relation to you.* Human beings are social; we are part of a group. And that is something we all relate to. All the time. Are you a biased vendor or neutral, hostile, friendly, how do the persons you are meeting assess your intentions and what's their premise that puts them in a certain position in the context of you. How are you regarded by the customer?
- *Preconceptions.* They already have or they are building them up

while meeting you, this is crucial to understand and manage in order to subsequently earn trust. You need to remove obstacles. One example is that they might have a preconception that you are not experienced enough, then deal with it, show them that it's wrong, or show them it's right but compensated for by other appreciated skills etc. Deal with it and do it in order to build a foundation of trust.

- *Sweet spots of interest.* You need to identify the keys that open mental doors. What are the person's interests? What is the person's disposition? How can you impress or awaken this unique human being? What impresses that person? What are the pain points that capture interest?

- *Emotional weather forecast.* What are the instant emotions commanding the behavior of the person you are meeting? This you need to pay constant attention to. They could change in microseconds. Rain can be replaced by laughter suddenly, or quietness and low energy could be aroused by triggers that you weren't prepared for.

- *Expectation management.* This is part of some of the other points but separated because you absolutely need to not only understand the expectations the customer is bringing to the table but more importantly how you manage them, since that is key to the experience later on. If the expectations for various reasons are too high, you will have challenges in performing and receiving higher feedback value from the experience. In contrast, if the expectations are low, you get the chance to overdeliver and subsequently receive better feedback from the experience. Even if your particular performance is similar in both scenarios.

- *Starting point for the Story Journey.* You need to find an entry, a door and a starting point for the educational story you are about to tell. That is the compiled conclusion from all the research you have been doing, most of it in real time, and it is a place and position from which the customer also gives you instant acknowledgement that it is the right starting position. Many times, it is a simpler level then you thought, a warm up phase into the topic, be nice and humble with your student. The starting point is like in the valley, looking up the mountain you are about to climb all the way up to the top.

These are all strong suggestions and tips on how to engage in the person you are about to educate, but it is always good when approaching another person, no matter the situation, to use this routine to check where that person is in a few mental aspects. It helps the communication in so many dimensions and becomes effective in new dimensions when applied.

Too fully see, engage and respect the person you are communicating with is a key differentiator in this world, please remember that. Most people think they do this, but they are only scratching the surface and never really see what is going on. This is about interest in the person you communicate with. This should be simple and natural because it is basic respect and fundamental in effective trust building.

FOUNDATION THREE – THE STORY JOURNEY

Now comes the fun part. Time to perform for real.

This is the phase of explanations, descriptions and pedagogic finesse. You take the customer and student by the hand and start walking up the hill or bring them on a flight or dive deep into the sea. You bring them on a journey with the purpose that they should encounter and discover parts and reach milestones that are all building up to the full picture, your painting of the topic. And for that I suggest a whole range of tools and skills you can apply. As most models and methods, they are not all or fully applied every time, but when you are aware of them and master them you can choose the ones that best suit the specific situation.

Sometime during the year, the Cassiopeia Star Constellation looks like the letter "W" on the Norther Hemisphere and that design of the "W" could also be the description of a *process*. That symbol value relates to the steps in the Story Journey and also the integrated approach to continuously working with various perspectives, star perspectives, and to a large extent contributes to the reasoning behind the term *The Cassiopeia Method*.

The Story Journey is built up by building blocks, and if you have been disciplined to The Cassiopeia Method from the beginning you already have the building blocks of the topic from the first part; The Content Basis. When you were building up the knowledge yourselves around the topic you identified the most important parts in order to be able to add the relationships and an effective perspective and how to explain it for an eight-year-old child. Those essential building blocks you need as milestones in the Story Journey in "the walking" together with the student.

You present or let the student explore each building block and connect them with the earlier identified relationships between the building blocks. And the reason I bring it all together and call it a "Story" is because I want it to bind together and the articulation of the jump from one building block to the next one should make sense, so that you can explain through the relationship how it all binds together. If you can describe it all in a drama story then fine, go ahead, but that is actually another skill. Story telling could be one of the most powerful ways of communicating with a human being, but it also requires another level of needs and skills on the part of the person telling the story. In this context of learning how to educate complex matters in a short format I leave that as a bonus track. Let's learn the basics of good explanations first.

The starting point is crucial and highly connected to the second part of The Cassiopeia Method: The Look. Ideally you see and understand and agree with the individual student on where to start, related to all the kind of parameters that are current and active at that moment for that person. Be crystal clear with the student that you are starting the explanation and a journey together and make sure the student is with you. I say that again; make sure the student is with you from the start. Sometimes that means that you take one physical step closer to the person, or you lean forward over the table, use your arms and hands to describe the starting point, catch the student's eye and agree with an acknowledgement that now you will soon have it all explained and you better be here and not somewhere else. Please, concentrate and focus on this topic just until we arrive to the final destination of the Story Journey. This moment, when you agree about the starting point and get the acknowledgement and focus of the student is not common practice in communication or presentation training sessions. But I can't stress enough the importance of making this communication of explaining complex matters at least somewhat interactive. And by "somewhat" I mean that you need acknowledgements over the course of the journey from the student that the building blocks and relationships are understood. Otherwise it will be hard or impossible to make the final big picture as impressive and full of enlightenment as it is supposed to be.

And to be over-clear with you as a student of The Cassiopeia Method; the Story Journey is a mental process; you take the student step by step until they see the big picture and have arrived at the next level of understanding. It is crucial that the first two parts are done well, The Content Basis and The Look because they tell you the milestones of The Story Journey, the starting point and suggest what tools you should use to clarify and simplify the understanding process. And those tools are presented in the rest of this chapter. There are many of them and they are almost never all used at the same time, you chose your weapon depending on the situation and the student. And some tools you just implement in the flow and apply for two seconds and then move forward. That is part of your skill as a presenter and teacher. When you know all the tools at hand you also get better and better in judging when to apply what. Also, this is my list of tools that I find effective and appreciated based on my experience. Of course, it is likely that there are additional effective tools to be used.

Nevertheless, I present them divided into parts, but they should be applied in a flow and integrated into The Story Journey. Although there are some tools that are more or less mandatory for the application of The Cassiopeia Method and they are; The Executive Summary Format, the journey process format and some of the tools for perspectives.

Picture 4. The Story Journey.

EXPECTATION MANAGEMENT – A PROFESSIONAL MOVE

One of the most underestimated forces when delivering something is *expectation management*. Highly related to the perceived outcome, a direct effect on the customer experience.

Vendors keep ignoring the fact that whatever they do or deliver will be compared with the expectation level the customer brought into the situation.

However, you can do something about this, you can manage the situation, and it is critical to be professional about this and act deliberately and in a skilled manner.

The sum of all interactions with a brand minus (-) the expectation level = Customer eXperience (CX)

Most or all of our time we keep working to develop and optimize the first part; every aspect of a customer's interaction points or touchpoints with the brand, making sure they have the best possible experience. The same goes for what we might deliver in various communication formats. Although it gets a lot more interesting when we start to manage the second part of the equation and set the right level of expectation.

Obviously, the first and often most instinctive thought is to lower the expectations as much as possible because then it will be much easier to overdeliver and achieve a higher CX result. That is partly true, but traditionally we have Marketing and Sales departments that are fully loaded and constantly fire off communication and fill customers with arguments, sweet talk and fancy campaigns that all raise their expectations to the sky and this makes it harder to deliver a great Customer eXperience. Why do they do that? Well, it is not that strange since we have a competitive situation. Brands are fighting for the customer's grace and that will keep driving the expectations up.

Good or bad, at least we have a greater understanding and awareness by knowing this and we can start working on a proper balance. And that is a job with expectations right at the beginning of our communication with the customer or student. Meaning, through different tactics we could communicate what the customer or student should expect from consuming this piece of content we offer. And since this book is mainly about educating and clarifying complex and complicated topics it is very effective to actually state that, communicate how hard the topic is and that it requires ambitious engagement from the student. The reason is very simple; when someone has said how tough and hard the topic is then *the experience* tends to be more positive when they actually *get it*, when they do indeed understand the topic.

But since The Cassiopeia Method is about building trust and a voice of authority, a teacher's voice, you can't manipulate expectation management either. That might otherwise be the temptation, but it would be counter-productive in the long run and also negative in so many other aspects as mentioned in this book. This is not the time or the context for more manipulation than we already have seen and experienced from the Marketing and Sales tradition, the new customer is too smart, insightful and has too many options to move on to someone else.

Here's the take-away from this sub-chapter: Be clear with the student about how hard the topic is.

Remember, The Cassiopeia Method is an application and practical implementation of Education-Based Marketing or Commercial Teaching or whatever you call it, and is not about product arguments or brand glamour, it is about a subject that the student should be given a chance to learn more about and that gets so much easier when you lower the expectations for this sub-activity of Marketing and Sales.

But again, it is crucial to stay loyal to the concept of being honest and trustworthy, the topic has to be complicated to be able to say that it is complicated. What would you expect?

Personally, I would also recommend sometimes adding some drama into the expectations, and that might seem odd at the first glance. But this is, at least a little bit of a story-telling situation, delivering the Story Journey. And in order to create an interesting narrative, you want the student to become interested and energized and want to know how this will all possibly pan out. From the world of creative writing I learned the difference between these two sentences:

- The dog sat on a carpet.
- The dog sat on the cat's carpet.

And that is how you with simple tools insert some drama, tension and interest into the situation. And that is something you could be creative about just before you are supposed bring the student on a Story Journey too. Don't just lower the expectations, change the direction of them, let them believe that it is pretty well impossible to explain a certain complex topic but that you are up for the challenge and intend to give it a go. Good luck, the student might think, and then eager to see if it is possible. They are exited but you keep the expectations fairly low.

Be aware of the possibilities you have to deliberately work with expectations and drama.

You didn't see that combination coming, right?

THE JOURNEY AND THE STORY

We have had story telling forever and it is widely known for its power to engage a human being. Almost like nothing else. It's part of the deeper needs of a human being; to being entertained, excited, interested, drawn away, be a part of something else for a while. The power of the story seems to be hardwired inside our body ready to become unleashed at any time.

As long as there is an initial connection, a start that is compelling, a bait impossible to resist, at a level suited to me. Then; take me away, let me come with you, Mr/Ms Narrator.

There is almost an innumerable number of books and content out there describing the world of designing good stories. That is not exactly what we are up to here. Only parts of it, and the reason is that in this case we have a significant learning situation which demand more of an interactive setup, at least an acknowledgement process in place. A storyteller in its purest format would rather like to tell the story without being disturbed by sudden clarification questions or acknowledgements. But we are bringing elements of a story into this, especially the quest to reach to a triumphant ending.

We have all heard from Marketing and Sales cliché statements like *You got to get into the mind of the customer* or *We need to understand the needs of the customer.* And yes, we have probably all said that ourselves too. I know I have.

That isn't enough anymore.

We have to do more and engage fully in the individual person's context and conditions. That is how you lay the foundation for creating this great customer experience. The journey starts with that individual's starting point, not the topic's starting point.

Take a moment and consider that.

This part is maybe the key to truly making use of The Cassiopeia Method. This is the biggest difference compared to most teaching, presentation skills and sales pitching.

The starting point is mentally and emotionally somewhere inside the human being you are addressing. The student, the customer, whoever you are communicating with and your ambition is to take that person on a short learning journey.

You often acknowledge that you are doing this by saying the starting point out loud using sentences that show that you are now in the world of that person. Could be a statement, an example, a situation, a feeling or whatever closely related to that person. This creates connection and engagement. Something that awakens from a potential sleeping mode or non-engagement mode.

No doubt we live in times of distractions. They have exploded and are everywhere. If we want to, we can be distracted at all times, every second we have left after we have focused on important or deliberate things. Those distractions could become an enemy for us teachers. It is of the utmost importance that we appreciate their existence and learn how to deal with them. How often have you been standing, talking to someone and suddenly a mobile phone rings and the moment is gone? Or people in meetings or larger group presentations who lose interest and start to work or engage in other tasks?

It is not enough anymore to just focus on the great topic, or look at the surface of the customer's interest.

You need to step right into the world of the student, grab their hand and bring them out on a trail. They go along because you are one of few who obviously really cares about and respects where they are coming from.

This means you cannot only focus on rational aspects, which most persons in a teacher's position do, because we are dealing with human beings. They are full of emotions, assumptions, opinions and colorful experiences. Additionally, you have the intellectual and rational point of view. You need to bring all those aspects into the search for an appreciated and effective starting point. Obviously, depending on the student or students, the journey begins in different places, but still you are telling basically the same story, but you might chose a few different paths along the way. This is news to many teachers, keynote speakers, bloggers and analysts. Although it seems simple and logical when you read about it here, it is most often forgotten about.

I keep reiterating the importance of being highly engaged in the mental and emotional journey of the student, and this is key to what The Cassiopeia Method is mostly about. Understand, see it, but then also align appropriate supporting techniques along the way.

To design the Story Journey in The Cassiopeia Method as part of an Education-Based Marketing initiative or base it on Customer Journeys could be a highly effective and successful approach but it can't be built on stereotypes, or being too standardized or completely predictable. It has to be *personalized*. This is obviously easier to do with one or five people, but how do you make this happen with hundreds of thousands or even millions of customers? Yes, that is when technology comes in to help us. There are tools to use and the development in this area is intense. And interesting!

I argue that the true personalized Story Journey as a teaching method is a crucial part of modern, effective teaching, part of communication and marketing. And I keep finding myself surprised that it doesn't seem be best practice in the market place.

The practice circulates around the topic and most of the time more or less from the teacher's point of view. This is an opportunity for all of us who want to do this in another way; *teaching with instant alignment*.

It's never black or white though, the good old teaching method does work on some occasions. With great presentation skills or writing skills or whatever other skill, a topic can definitely come out as entertaining and interesting. The question is whether it creates a deeper impact on the receiver or not. Did the communication actually change anything, does the customer want to actually act and buy now, did they understand enough to make it applicable in their situation? It is so much more interesting, elegant, sophisticated and effective when the receiver also gets to learn something. It could still be entertaining! Why shouldn't it all be entertaining?

Just as simple as that. Again, start from the position of the receiver, the student and/or the customer. Again, it is so powerful when you as a teacher really *see* the student. Use your imagination, intuition, experience, intellectual power and paint a picture of the physical and mental place that person exists in. Build up a sudden obsession around that individual person, find out about the level of that person's knowledge, insights. Level of maturity? How effective is the person at assimilating information? In what format does this person best consume new information? Pictures, action, words, audio, video etc. Where are the emotions for this person? When could this person be focused and concentrated? All those answers should (eventually) give you: the starting point. Where the Story Journey begins.

We are at the fun part. The moment when you conceptually grab the hand of the student and go out for a walk.

Think of that as a mental picture.

Be empathic, you are here to help, and the only mission is to help this person to learn this particular topic, the knowledge should stay on afterwards and the experience should be positive.

You want to add some real value to this person. And you want to earn appreciation, and if you are engaged in some kind of business and have commercial objectives you also want to earn *trust* through this activity.

Then, with that unique starting point, you guide the student through the terrain. If the student is a novice the walk might be easy at first, but sometimes you have advanced and experienced people to teach and then you need to take them over rivers quickly and through the jungle to the tougher parts, mentally – the content world of the topic.

Think about your teaching as a journey where you walk with the student from the starting point through the terrain, with stops, obstacles, check points, and with a clear goal where you can end up and reach the important conclusion, summarize and get the feedback from the student.

This "walk of learning" could be a customer meeting, a twenty-second content marketing piece, a blog post, a video instruction, a one-year training program, 30 minutes of keynote speaking or a one-hour lesson in a public school.

The starting point and the journey are very effective during one-on-one situations. I can sometimes find myself using this in ordinary customer calls any day and for whatever reason I need to explain something.

It is like a crystal-clear marketing story. With an interactive component.

The reason it is crystal clear is not because it is particular easy for everyone to always understand the topic, but because the story takes the receiver by the hand and decisively guides them forward and makes the experience and learning crystal clear. When you end up at the finish line you can look back and with the big picture understand what the story and journey was all about.

A crystal-clear marketing story for the specific customer, or the crystal-clear education context for the student if you will.

Let's take this down to some details and explain more tangibly how this works.

Now is the time to use what you learned in the first part of The Cassiopeia Method about The Content Basis. From that part, you have already carved out *Content Building Blocks*, the big obvious parts of the topic, simplified and not too many. Those building blocks are now the milestones through the Story Journey. Those building blocks are like the stepping stones appearing in the water enabling you to jump from one to another to get from one side to the other in the sea.

Keep the content building blocks in mind when you are walking ahead with the student, make sure they understand and see what every part is about before you move on to the next building blocks. Because you are also building a house: *the house of holistic understanding*. The building blocks are ideally build on top of each other and finally you will have constructed something and the student can see the character of the house, what it looks like, the big picture and where it is situated. A crystal-clear picture of the building.

Moving from one building block to the other takes an understanding of how the two building blocks relate to each other, otherwise it is hard to make sense of this Story Journey, it would only be about learning bits and pieces. The *Relationships* make the student see how the building blocks are connected and how they affect each other and are potentially related through processes. When leaving one building block and moving over to the next, it is then time to mention, explain and introduce the relationship and make it fit together with the next building block.

By doing this through the Story Journey you finally also get to use what you have prepared in the first part of The Cassiopeia Method: *The Context*, the big picture, how it all fits together as a "building", but also how this context relates in a world of other close contexts.

Present the bigger picture at the finish line and make sure you take a picture of the faces of the students when they "get it". This is when you get paid for the work you have put into this piece of communication.

But how about the individual vs the larger group? How can you adjust this kind of Story Journey for an audience of maybe thirty, hundreds or thousands of customers or students? When it is impossible to see all individuals. An obvious challenge, but you can approach that in a few different ways. Apart from technology being developed for bringing us magic, there is a whole chapter about that in this book, there are some additional suggestions too.

Let's say you have a school class of fifteen-year-olds, teens, you see them in front of you and you have a lecture where you are supposed to teach them a new concept within mathematics. Since you need to address a group and not an individual, you need to quickly identify some common qualities among the youths in front of you. Take a look at them, use your superpower sight and *see* them and start to think about what you know about them, what you have heard them talking about, imagine yourself getting into their heads and minds and look for the best possible starting point. Not like a generic marketing persona description five hundred million miles away from the customers, well hidden in a sub-department somewhere at a corporate HQ.

This still needs to be a real commitment, because when you are not able to get to know each person in the target group, you need to at least engage properly with the sentiments, emotions, intellectual maturity and willingness to be open and learn from the group, and sometimes you need to make assumptions. But make committed assumptions, no lazy generic thinking.

Personally, I love to add intuition into this moment, as additional help. First gather all kinds of impressions, learning and reflections – then you let your "gut feeling", the intuition or inner wisdom, decide where to start in order make the most compelling and interesting start.

If you don't trust in your good intuition, then stick to what you read, see, hear and experience.

Again, the start is crucial, it says everything about whether you are up for the task to bring them with you on the Story Journey by grabbing them by the hand, or if you instead are going to choose the standard teacher's way and start with whatever logical first step considering the topic to be at the center. If you chose to prioritize the topic, or in the commercial world, the product, you will on the other hand never lose the student because you never got them hooked in the first place.

Sometimes you hit it right on target and a whole group give you applause, but reality tells us that the expectations might not be that you succeed with every person in the group. There could be endless explanations why a certain person just won't be able to concentrate and digest what you are teaching on that particular day or at that particular moment. See the whole group as an upside and go for the majority instead.

If the goal is to really teach something that sticks and gets the students to understand, then you look for common denominators and a situation or context that might be compelling to most of the persons in the audience. The challenge with a group is typically to find the starting point that awakens and engages most of the individuals in the audience. Sometimes it happens and other times a great second outcome could be that you catch or grab the attention of some of the most influential students and they might awaken the others for you. When they understand, and see that not all the others have understood a particular topic, that hopefully makes them inspired to start teaching and tell others about the topic.

And just to be clear on the "hold by the hand part". During the Story Journey, it is crucial that you stop at the checkpoints, the building blocks and ensure clear acknowledgement that the students are following you. Don't accept a blasé *yes* as an answer to the question if they are with you so far, but also occasionally ask them to describe in their own words what they have learned and how they look at a certain part of the topic.

This is naturally not an easy task when it comes to digital marketing, let's say a customer is looking at an instructional video for three minutes, how do you have checkpoints during the way? Well, it might be hard to get the immediate response from the customer for each check point, but you as the creator of that piece of topic, having this awareness of the strengths of checkpoints built into the story, can address the receiver in the video with questions and challenge them to mentally go back and ensure their understanding of what was just explained. To create the acknowledgements in an artificial way and let the student repeat the parts they have gone through so far in the Story Journey.

The Story Journey is a great tool for anyone open to trying slightly new approaches to teaching and communication.

Are you with me?

THE EXECUTIVE SHORT SUMMARY FORMAT

The Executive Short Summary Format is a cornerstone of The Cassiopeia Method and completely aligned to the behaviors and needs of modern man.

Think *short* and *effective*, just like you do when you write an executive summary.

If you don't know what I mean by that, here's what I mean: The term "executive summary" comes from the need to provide the essence, summarizations, conclusions and recommendations of a topic, content, issue or whatever there is to be presented to someone who doesn't have the time to engage in the details and every possible aspect of a topic. And it probably needs to enable a decision of some kind.

Typically, this was done and still applies, in the business world for corporate executives where the executive summary is a condensed version of a larger report. It's related to the Abstract in the academic world but not exactly the same since the executive format is more of a mini version of a larger report and the Abstract more of an overview.

In the executive summary with a summarizing text, you express the most important parts, add a few suggestions for conclusions and sometimes options for decisions. And then you also have the whole report to back it up. Obviously, you need to describe the issues, the context, the possible alternatives to move forward in a very clear and comprehensible way and the prepared recommendations need to be thought through. It should be easy to quickly get an overall picture and then make the decisions. The whole point of the executive summary format is that it is extremely well prepared and aligned to the reader's situation with scarce time resources.

Why then is it so important to apply an executive short summary format in The Cassiopeia Method?

Firstly, I sometimes include the word "short" just to stress the importance of keeping most of what you do within the framework of The Cassiopeia Method in a short and crisp format. That's why I often express it as the executive short format.

Secondly, it is not only time that is the scarce factor here. It is just as much *mental bandwidth*. It's all connected to the modern situation with information overload and an extreme data explosion resulting in an impossible situation for most people when it comes to keeping up with everything that happens. You simply run out of bandwidth to be able to digest new information. You need to wisely choose where to put you focus and strength. That is why this format is so popular. When you are presenting your specific and maybe complex topic, it is highly appreciated if it is condensed and well aligned and you only provide the necessary details. You don't communicate the whole report, just the executive short format.

The factor *"time"* is one of the main reasons why this format of an executive short summary is important. Most people, not only corporate executives, are extremely short of time, most minutes are already booked for something, the mobile devices took the last couple of seconds waiting for the bus, train and even take time on airplanes. This makes this technique incredibly appreciated by all customer-facing professionals. Customers love it.

If you want to be able to get inside the head of a customer you need to learn how to respect the scarce resources in place, you need to respect the challenges each individual faces to engage in all possible aspects in life. Especially, if you have some sort of commercial intent and the person doesn't really immediately understand the context and value for precisely their unique situation, the probability is great that they zoom out and only give you a polite and artificial smile and decline further discussions.

To create an executive short summary format, you need to be effective with your words and always have in mind, always assume, that you are *communicating with smart and educated people, but explain as to someone who has forgotten the topic.*

This is key. This is a typical characteristic of The Cassiopeia Method.

I can't stress the importance enough.

This should be part of the DNA of a modern customer-facing professional to use when appropriate. Communicate short, effectively, aligned and respect the intelligence you are meeting, but still meet them at the beginning on the simplest level and move quickly forward into more complex matters.

The truth is, during most customer meetings there are topics and parts of the discussion that don't need to be lengthy, with all the details. Not even when the customer "gets it". Keep them on the hook and proceed in the Story Journey. Additionally, you can't expect them to understand things you haven't shown them or led them to, so you need to quickly *lead* them into the topic, often do some *fast repetition* of facts and information that are crucial but also standard and already known by most people, but may be forgotten by the individual you are communicating with in this fast-changing life. Fast repetition is often a highly appreciated technique.

I'll give an example of The Executive Short Summary Format, imagine I sell or market blinders that you put over your eyes while traveling, to shut out light to give you better preconditions to be able to sleep.

Are you a traveler who prefers to arrive in a fresh condition?

An exclusive blinder might be your best investment this year since good and consistent sleep is a major contributing factor to a healthy life.

It is all about creating darkness.

You might have forgotten it, but the reason we need to shut out light while sleeping is...the sun! And the fact that we are circulating around it. Yes, think about, the Earth takes 24 hours to turn around its own axis and during that time the sun is only shining on parts of the Earth at each and every moment, everything else is dark. Your part of the world is only lit up during a certain number of hours. And over thousands of years the human body has adapted to that. Thousands! And now we have an inner biological clock that determines how much each and every person needs to sleep every night, all connected to light, or actually to darkness. And here's the question: do you want to go against mother nature just because you're traveling on a plane with lights turned on and flashing video screens? And you also realize it might be impossible to make your teenage seat neighbor shut down their video screen. The answer and simple solution is a BLINDER, to artificially shut out light, to help nature, it all make sense, right? Takes two seconds to put it on, hello Darkness and then good night.

Order your own BLINDER today at www.blinders-goodnight.com and find them in your next airplane seat. Safe flight!

Pretty short, and effective. Explain, but not too lengthy, treat the student/customer as someone who actually already knows all this, you just give it to them again in case they forgot. You don't always need to spell it out as clearly as in this example above but if you have the right ambition and intent your receivers will appreciate the message that much more.

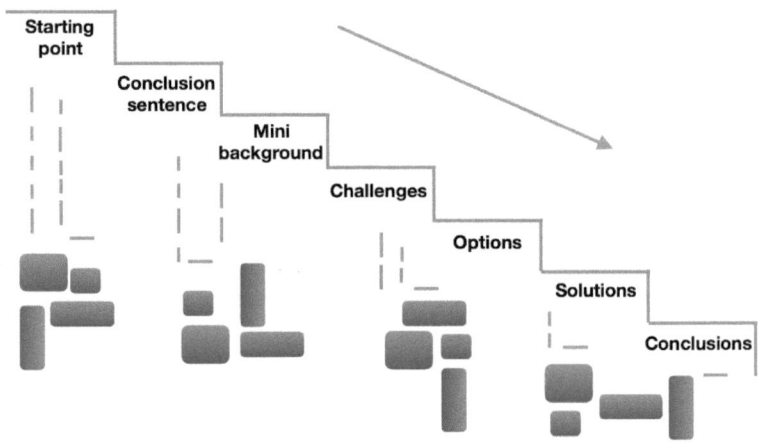

Picture 5. Building blocks, the Executive Summary Format.

In *picture 5* we see the building blocks of an effective executive format. And this works in all presentation formats; live on stage, in text, sound or video and animation.

The Starting point should be on high level, or at least tangible, interesting and create curiosity. And then it just keeps going in a fast, logical and easy way, it should be like walking down a stair. The starting point has an important effect since it needs to meet the receiver where the receiver is mentally, at the moment. That is not easy to figure out as you could read about in the other parts of The Cassiopeia Method, like The Look and the Story Journey. Don't start with where *you* are, start with where your *student* is.

After that, you state the *conclusion sentence* or sentences, and this part doesn't need to be complete or too informative, in fact I found out that it can be even more effective when you tease and build up the interest. You could consider what conclusion is the most thrilling and interesting and give that one away early. Similar to a classic cliffhanger.

Then you need to effectively give the student a chance to understand what this is about and that is why you deliver a shorter version of a background screening, a *mini-background*, building up the picture with important blocks as you learned in the Story Journey, things that it is vital to be aware of in order to see the big picture and see why it all ends up where it actually does end up. Be basic and clear on this, but always have the attitude that the receiver is smart and well educated.

State the *challenges* the topic has, there are always constraints and things that are considered as obstacles that need to be addressed, because if you don't bring it up the receiver will do it and you might find yourselves in a defensive position. Critical thinking is well developed and this is something you can foresee in order to keep the positive and professional level up. Sometimes the whole context is based on some problem statements, like in academic researches, then the challenges or problem statements need to be highlighted earlier, definitely before the mini-background.

The next part is about *options*. Everything is moving, which means that you almost all the time need to consider how to relate to a topic, sometimes that means making a decision, and sometimes it is just about deciding on your point of view. Clearly, this is about presenting various directions and ideally it all ends up in giving tangible suggestions for *solutions*.

A *solution* could be something you are selling or marketing but it could also be just the best available tangible approach for that context. Independent advisory is many times a better way to market than direct selling.

And then you provide the *conclusions* that are solid and sharp.

In total, this all might give the impression of being a lot, but it shouldn't. You as the provider of this need to have this as a mental framework and most importantly; the intention to provide something short and descriptive, highly aligned to the receiver. The exact steps described here are not mandatory, there could be any steps, but The Executive Short Summary Format needs to do the job of quickly bringing the topic to the receiver and leading them through the parts and ending up somewhere good.

Without losing the student, without losing the mental presence of the customer.

ZOOM IN AND ZOOM OUT

Here is another significantly strong teaching technique I use. It is as appreciated as it is simple.

It has a clear positive effect in opening up the mind, the eyes and can both increase the level of understanding quite quickly and decrease the time it takes for a student to *get it*.

The simplest example you can use is the one with a spaceship.

Articulate how the student arrives on Earth in a spaceship, entering our solar system, eventually getting closer to the Earth, seeing the whole globe. Coming from a wide perspective and narrowing down to first seeing the continents and then continually higher resolution of land and sea and eventually the details of Earth appear in full scale and finally you set the spaceship down in a specific place.

You might as well skip the spaceship in this example, and use the specific context, your teaching topic, and keep zooming in and zooming out until the student sees the context by themself.

Because this is mostly about getting a feeling for the context.

See the big picture, and then the small picture.

Think outside the box, and inside.

Grow things, maximize them, or minimize, take a step to the side and look into the topic, make space between yourself and the parts of the topic you are aiming at.

The same experiment in mental space could be effective in multiple situations to create distance to the immediate focus point and the surroundings and to set some perspectives on what we are talking about or experiencing. Most of the time you don't need to use the Sun or the Earth. More of different lenses for what you are teaching. You can use all kinds of dimensions, but the basic way of using zoom in and zoom out is to go from the details to the big picture and the other way around. Back and forth.

The movement is key.

Example: you might need to explain what a complicated technology product is about, and then instead of starting with the inner details of the product you can start with an everyday example where you use it, and you literary bring the student on a mental journey all the way down to the details, or back.

I prefer to make it visual, and I prefer to make it similar to a mini-journey.

This technique is recommended to combine with the Story Journey. It's highly effective "to arrive" at the starting point, but could just as well be used in the middle of the learning process or as "the last punch".

Keep your eyes on the mental state of your student all the way through the teaching part with *Zoom In and Zoom Out* and make sure the student is with you.

The *Zoom In and Zoom Out* technique is also an appreciated tool when it comes to reiterating a value statement, when it's necessary to give a reminder of and prove again the value and reason why something is valuable and good. Take a step back from the blurred situation and give the situation some perspective. And the smart usage of *Zoom In and Zoom Out* can clear most fogs and be the key to opening up a closed mental space in your and the customer's mind, or whoever's involved. Because you might start seeing new opportunities and options close to your situation when you step back, or up, and see the bigger picture.

Picture 6. Zoom In and Zoom Out.

INSTRUCTIONAL TEACHING VS PERSPECTIVE TEACHING

Interrogatives like *Why, What* and *How* might be overused in business literature but they are quite handy in order to discuss various types of Education-Based Marketing and Commercial Teaching or whatever way you chose to offer clarifications, education and enlightenment.

There are a number of ways of teaching, various *types*.

How teaching is applied.

You probably recognize most of them.

- Authority (lecture)
- Demonstrator (use experiments and examples)
- Facilitator (help for self-help)
- Delegator (collaboration, interactions in group format)
- Hybrid (a blended and integrated approach to teaching)

Obviously, the choice of teaching style or type could depend on many parameters such as the situation, the character of the individual students and the group, the topic and the size and ambition of the learning scoop and the strengths and weaknesses of the teacher.

You could respect the ancient Greeks' way of releasing critical thinking through debate and Q&A in the Socratic method and you can stand at the front line to the future and embrace the exploding innovation in Education Technology (EdTech) and Communication and Customer Technology.

Related to technology we can state there has been a substantial boost around *video* as a format. We have seen a proliferation of *Instructional Teaching* and that is mostly about the *How* and often tangible and more or less hands-on situations. How to make things work, how to precisely solve a specific problem, detailed instructions, easy to understand and copy. See and learn. Use your eyes, imitate the tangible actions and you have both solved your problem and learned something. And since it's most often a restricted situation, problem or challenge, it becomes easier to grasp and in some aspect, easier as a teacher or marketer to embrace and start building scenarios, training series, scripts, how-to-do-steps etc. Later, when you add presentation skills and apply the techniques within The Cassiopeia Method, the greater the probability will be that you succeed in offering consumable and appreciated pieces of educational content.

Although, I believe that teaching with the ambition to lift the level of understanding of the student on *What* or *Why* needs something more than instructions.

Since the *Why* often gets larger, deeper, more complex and blurred, other practices and techniques are needed. Obviously, when the abstraction levels and the intellectual requirements are more extensive, it is far easier to lose students on the journey towards the goal. And the *What* could be hard since it many times demands a decision; this is the place where the direction is chosen. This is the strategy and tactics decision phase, and when the context is complex this part is naturally hard. As soon as you move into the *How* phase everything becomes clearer, maybe not easy, but most often clear and fairly easy to work with since it is tangible.

The Cassiopeia Method becomes particularly useful in the pursuit of understanding complicated *Why* and *What* and lays the foundation for a more effective *How* phase.

With the ambition to distance oneself somewhat from the *Instructional Teaching* I call this other approach *Perspective Teaching* and I refer to the fact that it is often is more of a theoretical approach, but it doesn't need to be abstract. To meet the needs of a broader perspective to profoundly understand reason and effect and context. A built-in distance to the actual reality, the object we are trying to teach.

Why is this important to distinguish, why do I mention this?

The purpose is to clarify and make sure you approach different communication and teaching needs with the right kind of tool and mindset. Through experience, often in business and life, you are so much more effective, more often on target and successful when you know what you are doing, why you are doing it and how to approach it. Instructional and perspective teaching is preferable, a conscious choice. Zoom into the instructions and zoom out to provide the big view and perspectives.

Here is an example. You are searching the web for an instructional video about how to put up a blind in your bedroom. For this purpose, it is not likely or smart nor does it make any sense to provide teaching around blinds that presents the whole concept with various perspectives around blinds, their history and innovation journey, various industry developments and trends, playing around with zoom in and zoom out. Few are interested, because they know what a blind is, why you have it and just need to know how to install it. Perspective teaching would be off target, ineffective and make the student impatient. The consumer or student just wants to fix the problem: how to put up the blind in the window. An *instruction* is needed.

But in another example; a random marketer professional who might be supposed to build up a digital marketing campaign and has heard or seen from colleagues that he or she should use a new software product that automates certain parts of the campaign and visualizes everything. But he or she as a marketer just doesn't have a clue what the product really is and does, except for automating, and how it might fit in to his or her specific situation and conditions. In fact, the marketer has to state that he or she isn't an engineer and doesn't really know much about technology. In this case, you need to quickly put the product in a comprehensible context, defuse and explain and paint the big picture, describe where marketing and technology comes from, what it might do for a marketing department, the value it brings – simply put it into a perspective that helps the marketer to start to see the product as one part in a larger map. When the *Perspective Teaching* is communicated, and accepted, then all options are open for the marketer to proceed and receive more *instructional teaching* to see more of the details of the exact function of this piece of software.

To be able to provide *Perspective Teaching* you can obviously use techniques in The Cassiopeia Method like; Zoom In and Zoom Out, The Perspective Towers and The Swedish Perspective.

PERSONALIZE THE CONTENT WITH PERSPECTIVE TOWERS

While engaging further in The Cassiopeia Method you sooner or later probably want to learn more about how exactly to get started. How to do this. How to explain something complicated and ensure the receiver understands.

Apart from seriously recommending that you engage in a structured way and follow the three big blocks of The Content Basis, The Look and The Story Journey there are some significant compelling ways to prepare the content and venture into The Story Journey.

Choose a smart and effective *perspective* based on what terminology and pictures that work with the target group or the individual you are communicating with.

Yes, a *perspective*.

A context. A subject matter point of view. A geographical, cultural, political, business or historical situation. A feeling or philosophical or physiological approach. Or whatever colors or theme of words you choose. The *perspective* is your key. Your way into the world of *personalization*. It's your opening line and scene. It's through the *perspective* you calibrate with the student to end up on the same wavelength.

The beginning of communication that works.

Obviously, a group of fifteen-year-old boys in Italy might need one set of perspectives they understand and relate to and probably, older women in the UK have their own usable perspectives. It doesn't need to be as predictable as this, but when you start to know your group of students you'll soon find the right perspectives to start out with.

Perspectives are pretty much my personal secret formula, in many aspects the secret formula of living life. And I find this very useful in so many situations, especially when designing and delivering in communication that is well suited for the application of The Cassiopeia Method. In numerous other situations; both in my profession and also in contexts of more private nature.

Nevertheless, I realize my personal secrets are not so secret anymore since I have been fascinated enough by perspectives that I also wrote my first book about them. Actually, that book was only about perspectives with the question why we so often lose our perspectives and start making things harder than they really are. (*Varför gör du det så svårt för dig? En liten bok om perspektiv*. Moonred Media, 2015 – Why are you making it so difficult for yourself? A little book about perspectives.)

In that book, I introduced *The Towers of Perspective*: The Universe, Philosophy, Science, Religion, Music, Humor, Fiction, Time and Rules. They are called *Towers* because you should climb your way all up to the top of the tower where you can see the extent of a situation and a context and landscape, get the right perspectives of where you are and where you are heading. And accept the proper dimensions of various things happening, and not overvalue or underestimate or let whatever unbalanced judgement governs your decision making or instant opinions.

Example, in order to better understand a certain part of our rational world of reality you might want to take a detour into the world of fiction and that might help you better understand the fixed structure of reality when you come back. Or when you are supposed to learn about a new computer programming language it could be an effective tool to describe it in terms of creating music; in the structures, tones and themes.

Pick a perspective and start to create the content structure from there. This is obviously also one of the most effective pedagogic tools I've got. Use the perspective when applying the other technique *Zoom In and Zoom Out*. The combination is dynamite. And paint the picture with parables and images. Create and use content the student will be able to *see*. Use all the visual gifts you have.

SEE THE STUDENT AND THE CUSTOMER FROM A SWEDISH PERSPECTIVE

What is a *Swedish Perspective?*

Honestly, there could be many answers to that question (approximately ten million – the number of Swedish people), but in this context I use it as to describe a specific *approach and a point of view.* Used to address a customer or a student.

The *Swedish Perspective* is an attitude of being adaptive and aligned, to elaborate on a built-in way of being quickly adjustable according to larger elements. A natural and smart way of smoothly blending into the reality and acting on it, constantly producing value and ensuring that one remains appreciated. Always deliver with a true "Lutheran Nordic work ethic". Watch, learn the game, and act.

I am fully aware, sometimes painfully, that this isn't always considered to be great and helpful behavior, because you can easily fall into the trap of not having your own clear agenda, that you can't apply rule-the-world-leadership and end up not building your house on your own beliefs etc.

There are pros and cons with everything.

Sweden is considered to be a smaller nation, at least in number of citizens, and in modern times we have developed an impressive culture and behavior around being fast to observe and adapt to the larger global world and being productive about it.

Positive or negative, all opinions and both sides of the coin are constantly discussed, mainly by Swedes, but there are obviously some upsides and especially the capability and skill to really *see* what is going on in the world, from an outsider's perspective, a Nordic eye towards regions like the US, the UK, Germany, France, the whole Asian territory. But basically, the whole world. Swedes seem to have the gift of seeing what is needed and inventing, adapting, engineering, producing and exporting whatever is asked for. Most famous might be music, cars, furniture, industrial manufacturing, athletic accomplishments, clothing and technology. About technology; there is an endless stream of Startups within technology, which is also the case for many other countries, but Sweden keeps producing *Unicorns,* startup companies reaching a billion dollars in revenue. The Startups come in every color and version: within gaming, music, finance (FinTech), education (EdTech), biology (BioTech) etc. Armed with great combinations of skills, work ethics and superior capability to smartly position the products and solutions on the global map and maximize the service needed.

Swedes knows how to use a gifted eye for global perspectives. This book is actually not about Swedes or Sweden; it is about the behavior and skills.

To watch, analyze and always value the observations in a productive and street-smart way, and in total absence of restricting principals of pride and tradition. It sounds sad, I agree, but it is not what it looks like. Sweden have tons of traditions and pride in their country but never seem to let them become obstacles.

The *Swedish Perspective* doesn't stop at superior skills in observing and analyzing behavior, trends and needs in the world. Again, this is also combined with extreme work discipline and focus. It comes from a long history of hard work, probably on account of the hard winters which would literary have let you die if you didn't do the work properly and fill your barn with seeds and corn. Be careful about costs, make sure you keep savings, invest for the future. And many did die, if not through the tough winter, it was illnesses, wars or lack of food. And if you add to this a Lutheran attitude that celebrates silence and unrelenting work you've got the loyal Swedish worker. Eventually Swedes were lucky to have found engineering as their other gift to the world; the rational human being thrived and developed into a respected and appreciated global citizen.

What's with all this?

You can use this when practicing The Cassiopeia Method. Not least as the great *reminder* about being observant and keep attention levels up, leaving the restricting pride principals out of the way for a while and focusing on winning the game. Remind yourself while communicating: use the *Swedish Perspective.* Assimilate all impressions and transform them into productive actions.

My experience from effective teaching is that it comes from the ability to truly observe the students or customers, and to adapt to the given conditions, to bring in all important aspects of a situation and make that the starting point in the way you plan for the teaching and learning journey; the way you design a crystal-clear marketing and teaching story.

A *Swedish Perspective* is just a term for being observant and ensuring that you act on it, deliver on it. Teaching or marketing shouldn't always be about my way or the highway, it should be about a true relationship, an alignment with the recipient. To be able to accept the need to embrace a large portion of humility and openness and that doesn't always come naturally for people and brands, and I would argue that being humble in this context is smart and aligned to a future where the customers strengthen their power position.

IN-FLOW-REPETITION

Repetition is a well-known learning technique to ensure that knowledge sticks and stays in your mind, when we hear and digest a specific part of a topic a couple of times it makes all the difference, especially when it is a fact or piece of information considered to be very interesting or compelling for us.

From a teacher's or a marketer's or a customer-facing professional's perspective, when you are planning a lesson or a content marketing set or a dialogue structure, it forces you to clarify what it is you really want to stick with the student or the customer. What is it specifically that they should bring with them and remember from the lesson or marketing piece? What is it that they should be able to refer to or use and apply.

This might be the most concrete results you can expect. This is something you actually can measure, it is like an intellectual product you deliver to the receiver's brain. There is a huge difference between *education-based* and sales pitching, entertainment or marketing awareness, advertising. You actually want to achieve something at the receiver's level of understanding, let them learn something they remember and might be able to apply in their forthcoming life and probably in their decision-making processes. This is why it is so important to deliver something when you are practicing The Cassiopeia Method and the repetition highlights those pieces and lets you see what important parts you should further highlight and incorporate in repetition patterns.

When you have identified what parts you want to apply in your repetition you need to plan for it, to design the repetition, to make sure it becomes materialized in the communication. To basically go through the scripts and underline the most tangible value you bring from the lesson to the student or customer. The easiest way is of course to make sure a term is said three times, that might be better than nothing. But it is more powerful and effective, and also show your professional ambition, when you build the term and message into a couple of examples and contexts, and then later in the teaching journey you refer back to what you learned earlier, and now with the term in another context. This is very powerful.

Repetition is also extremely effective and useful when you are building up a case, a model, a complex context or whatever complicated situation you are trying to explain. Repetition is then like using building blocks. If you first go through the basics and then move forward to the next level, you continually go back to the prior parts and mention them in flow, *In-Flow-Repetition*, and you then ensure they won't be forgotten and you also ensure they are understood in the larger context. To secure the house you build is complete with all its parts, with sustained quality, all the way up to the roof. It is a natural part of the blocks and relationships build this into The Story Journey, inherited from the work within the phase of The Content Basis.

In fact, *In-Flow-Repetition*, not only repetition, should be incorporated as best practice in all good teaching.

OPEN UP CLOSED DOORS WITH HUMOR

I don't believe *Humor* is the right word or description of what ought to be applied in this context, since you still need to stay true to your serious brand and trustworthiness. In Swedish, there is an expression "glimten i ögat" that is exactly what I recommend. It can be literary translated to "a twinkle in one's eye" and what I am looking for is a soft, warm and kind approach to the application of humor, an intellectual eye opener with a twist – and not the obscure, ironic and black humor that you might find on TV-shows and practiced by stand-up comedians. I love that humor too, but everything has its place and I wouldn't recommend it in this context of teaching that should be built on trust. The risk is too high that it will be misunderstood and leave the customer with confused emotions. But that shouldn't, on the other hand, make you too scared so that you leave it all out and stay hundred percent stiff and overly serious, because when you dare to use some balanced and kind humor you also show you are confident in the situation, that you own the topic well enough to risk your own pride, evergreen advice is to not take yourself too seriously, provide some humble laughs and de-mystify the situation. But don't toy with the respected and trusted relationship.

Humor is nothing other than a great tool when educating since it can help you to open doors.

Actually, it is a great door opener.

Because a person who is insecure or afraid might be scared of being exposed as not having really understood and that could manifest itself in defensive and covert behavior. Then a non-threating style with a smile and a few humble jokes could open up and the person could become much more receptive. In a classroom situation, it can help the most defensive audience to cheer up, to open up. And this could be as effective when you engage one-on-one and through kind mini-jokes and empathy you could almost see in front of you how the individual student lowers their guard and becomes engaged. A student adapted to a more relaxed approach to the topic and learning process. Referring to the construction of our brain, this is a way to decrease the influence from the *amygdala*, the sensor for threats that could make us focus too much on flight or attack and not the ideal place you want to be if you want to learn something new and possibly quite complicated matters.

Thus, build in jokes filled with empathy and love instead of sarcasm and irony, just to optimize the learning situation, creating smiles and perspectives. And it makes it all so much more enjoyable. For you too.

Basically, it makes the whole learning process delightful, and it is obvious how much better you actually learn when you are enjoying the consumption of all new information.

Smile!

PLAY INTELLIGENCE IN TEACHING

Among all skills and techniques you could equip yourself with, this is a personal favorite: *Play Intelligence*.

Let me explain what I mean by *Play Intelligence*.

It is originally a term from the sports world, and many times it is looked upon as a gift, a natural born gift. To have superior *Play Intelligence* or *play understanding*. When I use these terms they typically come from team-based sports like football (soccer). In Swedish, we actually have a great word for this: *spelförståelse*, and a suitable translation would be something like *understanding of the game mechanics*.

The skill is all about the capacity to *see, feel and judge* how the game and situations are quickly developing and understand how to act on the ever-new current and upcoming present time (almost like the Swedish Perspective).

Great players can *read* their opponents and their own team members, and see the movements in the two teams, see them like living patterns, almost as if from above, to see the movements materialize. Be able to predict the next most possible move and take a position to prepare for that and potentially act on it. This skill applies to any player on the playfield, it doesn't matter if they have the ball (still with football as the example, in the real world the *ball* would be the *initiative*) or if they don't have possession of the ball. But the most significant *Play Intelligence* situations are when players actually have the ball and create something for their team, based on how the game is characterized on that special day and at that moment.

This skill and capability is even more beautiful in real life, outside sports games. And I don't believe it is only a natural born gift, on the contrary, it can be learned quite easy.

You can apply play understanding or *Play Intelligence* everywhere, and it should not be about being manipulative, it should be about being smooth and smart, if you ask me. When you see pattern in groups, situations and individuals it is much easier to align and create the results you want with less friction. Think about walking through a crowded grocery store, your only mission is to pick up some milk, eggs and bread, and when you start *seeing* your fellow human beings, your friends in the store, how they act and their movements it is much easier to achieve your goal which might be to move through the crowd as fast and efficiently as possible and make the purchase you planned.

In teaching situations, this is an underestimated skill and practice. Most of the time because the teacher or marketer isn't aware of this concept and doesn't know how to be conscious of *Play Intelligence*. All groups are built up of unique individuals, and every day is a new day and never happened before. It is crucial to be awake and see the special movements in that current context and adjust to them. *Adjust.*

Although, in teaching situations it is not only about the physical appearance, no, it is many times rather about *seeing, considering and judging* what is really happening in the students' minds and their emotional reactions and levels of concentration or distractions. Even if you have a grand standard plan for how to educate it becomes so much more effective when *Play Intelligence* is applied, because situations happen or appear all the time and they need to be addressed. All those instant movements when something unplanned crops up, that is when you need to quickly see that and act on it with the higher purpose in mind. Keep focusing on the game, manage distractions in the audience, or even use distractions as a tool for educating etc.

You might sit in deep conversation with a customer and you have it all figured out with The Cassiopeia Method. You are half way through the Story Journey of a very complicated matter and the customer is still on the hook and seems to be able to follow through all the way to Nirvana, hallelujah and the gold medal for now truly understanding this strange topic (where you, by the way, have some great solutions to offer). But all of a sudden, the customer seems distracted, you are not sure why, it could have been the text message on the phone that just beeped or the person previously walking by the conference room. But since you recognized a potentially negative distraction in the customer's mind you stop the Story Journey, right there and then. Time to check and see if there is something happening and if the customer wants to clear it up. A very direct way of managing the situation. But no matter whether the customer chose to deal with whatever distraction there might have been or not, the upcoming and last part of the intellectual walk through The Story Journey will probably be much more focused than if you hadn't slammed on the breaks.

We experience a huge wave of technology innovation around Artificial Intelligence (AI), where a lot of personal interactions and communications between a machine and a human being are developed to work at scale to be able to adjust to each and every individual person. Fascinating ambition and I am sure we will be surprised how useful this might be, but still, capabilities like *Play Intelligence* have been a superior gift for human beings, an *intuitive intelligence*. I would argue that when it comes to education it also takes *empathy* to be really effective and applicable. To create a safe environment for the student. I continue to argue that every form of manipulation will eventually be outvoted by human beings, and I can't wait until the customer power forces use global hyper-competition to checkmate manipulation.

Honest, smart and smooth *Play Intelligence* is something else, it is an effective tool to align to upcoming and often unplanned situations in order to keep focusing on delivering a great customer experience. Mostly in real time.

PRESENT, PUBLISH AND BE EDUCATIONAL WITH FINESSE

When teaching within The Cassiopeia Method, either through one-on-one Commercial Teaching or one-to-many Education-Based Marketing at scale, there are some obvious common denominators with compared with presentations skills and presentation techniques.

I can't remember how many presentation training programs I have done in order to improve presentation skills and acting on stage with the objective of communicating and creating a living and credible relationship with a live audience. There is an endless number of great suggestions, recommendations and tricks on how to prepare and consequently and ultimately apply smart techniques to win the audience's attention, respect and love.

Obviously, a few of them you should copy into the role of the teacher. Possibly, you might even consider applying most of the techniques if they make sense to you, they often do.

But within the art and techniques of live presentation I often lack one big part: how to be truly *educational*. How to apply the science of didactics. Teaching technique. Make the teaching stick. How to be an effective teacher. How to best describe a topic and make sure the audience really understands. I don't mean how you create a perfect presentation slide deck with optimized color settings and number of letters per slide or how my physical appearance is looked upon by the audience. How I should not cross my arms across my chest, excuse myself or not talk too fast. Optimization of my appearance as a teacher or presenter.

The Cassiopeia Method is more about the student, the customer, the receiver. That's the big point.

I mean how to align the mental journey of the individual in the audience, and not only by *winning* them over to become satisfied and entertained, but by ensuring that they actually absorb, digest and understand what is being said. This brings us back to the other techniques I have recommended; with the *journey* and finding the appropriate starting position, taking the student by the hand and leading him or her through the terrain of uncertainty.

If you are capable of doing that and at the same time applying all the great keynote speaker skills you have learned, then you have something extra to offer.

Thus, as a keynote speaker you have an opportunity to stand out, not only by being appreciated for entertainment, but to deliver educational finesse and not have the starting point in yourself but in the audience. This is for those who want to reach the next level of great speakers, to stand out. Chose a starting point, apply play intelligence in the room, be present and interactive and offer journeys with repetition, and continuous acknowledgement that the message is being properly received. From most presentations and keynotes, the audience leave the room with a certain feeling, was it good or bad, fun or boring, interesting or flat etc. This is where you want to stick in their minds for the right reasons, a clarified view of an interesting topic you just taught. By applying The Cassiopeia Method and focus on the core messages and value you want the listener to bring out of the room with new insights and learning for their specific world and context, not only short-term entertainment and feel-good emotions.

And giving a keynote presentation is just one format, this could and should also be applied in other content marketing formats like publishing a text, blog, white paper, book, advertorial etc. Being a customer-facing professional or marketer and being able to act as an empathic teacher and deliver it with superior educational finesse is exactly what the world of Sales and Marketing needs. For the simple reason that the new world is customer centric!

If your intention is to establish relationships built on trust, then stay away from manipulation.

I keep coming back to this, so no surprise that I advise you to always stay away from that.

Although knowledge on how the brain works and being able to take advantage of it could be a thin line to manipulation, but the important aspect of that is what the intention and reason behind it is. And if that is still to honestly provide improvement for your customer and student then it is fine. Because with some awareness of the learning process in the brain you can become more effective with the communication and you are able to avoid the worst scenarios. Your knowledge on how the brain works becomes the tool.

The science of the brain is a vast topic and I have no intention to cover it in detail in this book, I'll just mention and pinpoint some important parts close to the learning process. If you want to really learn more about the details, please expand your literature list and further engage because it could be very useful. And fascinating.

Learning and teaching without outlining what we know of the brain would leave us with a feeling that something is missing. The scientists are pretty well aware of the basics of the brain. Even you and I probably know the most foundational parts. Like the two big parts of the brain; one "logical" and one "creative". And before we move on to other important parts we can stay with these two sides. They are effective to switch between and apply different kinds of teaching approaches and experiences since all students are different kinds of human beings, all with their own setup in the brain and with varying gifts concerning ease of understanding logical arguments or receiving emotional input, texts or pictures etc. This means that if you can change the way you project and teach, the greater the probability is that you achieve a broad understanding in a group of students. That is why it is tremendously beneficial to use various kinds of techniques within The Journey Story; Zoom In and Zoom Out, Humor and Perspective Towers etc. in order to experiment with text, speech, emotions and pictures.

Talking *about* mathematic could be more effective towards achieving understanding for some people and for other people it is better to *concretely calculate* the numbers.

Another effective teaching technique related to how the brain works is to use pictures, situations and examples the student recognizes. Something familiar since that uses the synapse systems in the brain. They are built up from experiences, and they make it significantly easier and faster for a student to connect the new information in a context and embrace the understanding. Like if you are trying to explain for a child what a powerful dynasty was back in time and you describe parts of it like an anthill with the queen, workers and soldiers, a society construction and enemies. Then the probability is greater that the child gets it. Same for grown-ups, why don't you try to explain invisible sound waves in the air with the real waves on the water coming from a stone you just threw out in the sea. Splash! Water waves emanating from the center. Just like invisible sound waves reaching the ears.

This is partly the reason why Perspective Towers are so effective.

By the way, those synapse systems are ever growing and disappearing, that's why we have learned it is good to keep up the practice and exercise the brain, which means that it is a great idea to keep the synapse systems healthy and growing. And research around *Neurodidactics* tells us that multimodal ways are the best way to achieve this. In plain English, use different ways of teaching and learning. As with the two halves of the brain; use pictures, texts, experiments, physical motion, video etc. Literally, if you aspire to become a highly-sophisticated teacher, you could build up the synapse systems deliberately early on in your teaching in order to use them in a later part of the teaching. In an advanced course on The Cassiopeia Method I would teach how to build in the synapse potential right into The Story Journey.

Other important functions in the brain is the existence of the *hippocampus* and *amygdala*.

The *hippocampus* part of the brain represents joy; it's where we are more open and receptive to learning new things. This is obviously the place you most of the time want to be in a normal teaching situation.

With *amygdala,* we encourage flight and survival and don't learn openly and freely, we mainly focus on what can help us in a specific and dreadful situation. Still, I would argue that this could also be a highly interesting teaching and learning state of mind although it takes some thought and care to get it right. I am interested in using the extreme concentration that comes for example with fear. Although I haven't found many good situations in which to explore true fear, it might work occasionally with children in a school class, learning how basic behavior and rules have to work, otherwise… But with a customer? No, I can't find the proper use case, and it might be a good sign. Even with children it is probably a failure if you have to resort to fear.

Or maybe, you might connect fear as a result of being afraid to fail, which is a common fact.

The message needs to be succinct and of clear and useful value. Many people, fully pumped with stress hormones even in a normal day, would be those you need to consider as being in the amygdala place when they are supposed to learn something you are trying to teach them.

Stress. And then when you make the circles and examples too wide and too ambitious the student won't be able to concentrate. A stressed student is only interested in surviving and just needs minimal information in order to do that and then they just want to proceed in life. In order to respect that and be effective in your teaching results this needs to be considered when you analyze the student situation when starting up the lesson. Use your Play Intelligence.

As you can see, with some knowledge of how a human being works, how the basic brain functions behave, you can make some smart decisions on how to approach in a teaching scenario.

Picture 7. Learning process in the brain.

TEACHING VS PITCHING

Let us explore the fascinating distinction between teaching and sales pitching.

It's obvious and at the same time not obvious.

Both are trying to sell something.

Traditional teachers might disagree at first, but the fact is that they are all selling a story, selling pieces of information and knowledge and they want the student to buy it. The topic itself.

The Sales professional also sells the story but eventually and more important another product or service.

A sales pitch is pure and delimited communication content trying to inspire and convince the receiver to buy a specific product or service. Often built up by strong sales arguments why you should buy it.

Probably the biggest distinctions between a sales pitch and teaching is the *intention* and how important the core teaching content is to be received and understood. The intention of a sales pitch obviously has strong commercial flavors. The dream case scenario for a sales pitch is that the receiver gets so excited about the sales pitch that he or she bring out their wallet immediately, they want to buy what is being sold. A sales pitch is pivoted to a transaction, a commercial deal, a buying activity. And with that clear intention you also understand that a sales pitch is built up to convince you in the best and optimal way to go and buy and complete the transaction.

Teaching a topic could be something else. Well, yes, all teachers are selling something too, the topic. But they are not selling a product or service with a price tag afterwards. It means that the way of teaching doesn't need to be built up with that intention, with the arguments lined up in order to make the student go and buy something. The teacher could be more focused on the topic itself.

First and foremost, I want you to be aware of the distinction between the two ways of communicating, where both claim to teach.

With The Cassiopeia Method I want you to combine the two kinds in order to make the teaching more objective oriented and the sales pitching more trustworthy.

But first, let's go further into the two disciplines and the blur we might experience listening to teachers and sales professionals.

Sales pitching in the disguise of teaching is not always something you detect or think about, because no one ever tells you that they are going to deliver a sales pitch, they just do it. And then it is just that feeling afterwards, when you have consumed a piece of so-called teaching but there was something that wasn't quite right. You can feel it, sense it. You might have experienced a moment of sales pitching, and it doesn't matter if it is a person delivering it, or a piece of video or text, your internal trust alarm is evaluating the trustworthy level of the content and investigating if there are any threats to consider. Obviously, there are rarely any threats around sales pitching, but your body treats the situation the same way, it is the same evaluation process. You know why? It could be because someone is trying to manipulate you, steer you in a certain direction, convince you about something, trying to argue or relate to your feelings, maybe trying to scare you or attract you, before you understood it and agreed to it.

Most of the time it is someone who obviously is too subjective, engaged, passionate and eager to sell something to you. Could be anything, it doesn't need to be a product you should buy, it could be ideas and topics about anything in life and the society. Politics, maybe. But when a topic is fairly new to you and the communication is more about arguments rather than understandable explanations it can easily become blurred and unclear. The communicator might however argue they are just teaching to clarify the facts.

But as stated already, the underlying intention is the huge difference and also the structure of the communication.

When we look into the structure of a sales pitch we see how it is more about providing arguments in a nice way along the journey, leading the listener to a certain point where it is obvious that what is sold is something great and that you need to seriously consider to adapt. *Hey, if you don't get this you are the only one in the world! It is obvious, this is something GREAT.* It is secondary whether the listener has reached a higher understanding or not. The whole setup is more about the so-called teacher's planned process with the objective of winning a new customer, or winning someone to their tribe of believes.

Sadly, manipulation is still an effective tool when you are selling short-term products or contracts. However, since we now have this new powerful Customer, both smarter and equipped with multiple alternatives we will hopefully see more of non-manipulative selling and teaching.

This takes time, also because many sales professionals are hardwired with arguments and programmed as professionals to win over a person's opinions to their side, they often have huge challenges to hold this back. In order to deliver The Cassiopeia Method and in order to claim trust, Sales professionals need to adapt some aspects of discipline and take care of their obvious intentions and focus on their students. They still have their sales objectives, they won't go away, but they need to check out the sales pitching at the door for a moment when teaching and communicating with a vulnerable student and potential customer who has opened up and is ready to receive, it is a moment where you need to be careful otherwise the door will close again, and that might happen fast and it could remain closed for a long time. The sales pitching is an important skill saved for another part of the customer buying process, when it is appropriate, when the customer wants and needs to hear the arguments why they should buy a certain product. The challenge for Sales and Marketing departments is that they are often singing the same tune all the time and it is just not effective when you are trying to teach something and aspire to offer healthy Content Marketing and Education-Based Marketing in order to attract a new audience and establish trust and a long-term relationship. If you do that work well, in the beginning of the buyer's journey, if you build some kind of relationship where you have delivered great teaching, then you have the lead compared with the competition. Then the sales pitch comes naturally in the process of choosing the best product and vendor.

The same goes for marketers used to building in features and unique functions into their pieces of content, everything that can help build brand-unique parts with certain characteristics. This is also something that will be detected by the customer. My recommendation is to hold back a bit with these arguments and fully engage in more of objective teaching, the consumer will assimilate and consume the information more willingly. The sales and marketing aspect comes with the fact that you are doing this; delivering the education, showing you are the sponsor, you are the one engaging and investing in this training. The consumer sees that and mostly appreciates it when you show that there is a clear distinction between when you are more objective or more subjective. Needless to say, the consumer understands that there are commercial interests too and that you have a list of arguments around why you are the best in certain situations. The Customer becomes smarter and smarter. Nevertheless, stay calm and trust in the fact that everything has its time and place. This is the discipline that only some brands practice but they are treated with respect and it is beautiful to see.

Remember, replace classic manipulation with *commercial empathy* and customers will reward you.

What about traditional teachers, wouldn't they learn more about teaching with clear objectives to sell something? Well, for sure there are aspects of sales pitching that would be useful within teaching too. In the next chapter, we look deeper into teaching with commercial objectives.

TEACHING BASED ON COMMERCIAL REASONS

The Cassiopeia Method is intended primarily for professionals in customer-facing situations, some parts of Content Marketing, and as a starting point for algorithms, chatbots and Artificial Intelligence (AI) applications. But it is obvious that there are always aspects of commercial reasons closely connected to what is taught.

The built-in purpose of The Cassiopeia Method could be described in commercial terms. In some sense, the teaching is just a means to an end, a tool to achieve something else.

But instead of going straight into the sale, to the closing moment with *Say YES if you want this,* you go through Trust. The Cassiopeia Method should first get you to the position that you need to deserve it, not that you can force the customer or student to agree on it. Either they trust you or not, and most of the times they won't tell you which.

Oddly put, but basically *with The Cassiopeia Method you are selling Trust.*

Then, when you deserved that sell, you could move on with the sales pitching in order to keep competition away etc.

A company has business objectives, aiming for revenue growth, cost reduction and customer loyalty. Non-profit organizations often raise money to help out in a certain area and for some non-profit organizations the teaching and enlightenment is the core purpose.

The Cassiopeia Method serves all the basic reasons behind business and organizational objectives and this is what makes this form of teaching and marketing so interesting, it is rather sophisticated, because if you intend to succeed with this you can't only be rational and business driven, you also need to have the empathic people skills. Remember the important second part of The Cassiopeia Method about The Look? The student and the customer in the center focus, not always the topic you are teaching.

The same goes the other way around, with pure teaching practice you can't just dive into the topic, and forget that you are selling something, even if it is only the topic itself you are selling; it's helping you to be clear on why you teach a student or potential customer.

The Cassiopeia Method is also valuable to add to a superior Customer Experience, CX, you are honestly helping the customer to understand before they might even have bought the product. It is a great start on a customer experience journey.

Earning trust often comes through the work of engaging customers, increasing their awareness, preparing them for owning the product, sharing your expertize knowledge. Deliver it with quality to establish customer loyalty and lay the foundations for a profitable customer buying products over time. That's the hard-core commercial reasons behind this kind of teaching. But you should try to distance yourself from these strong basic reasons when you are delivering teaching, and excluding sales pitching in the educational content, it suffices that you as a company are standing behind and sponsor in the lessons.

The teaching techniques are also aligned and crafted to suit the modern and distracted customer described as being fast and effective, since modern customers have limited time and mental bandwidth. Nevertheless, this still makes those techniques highly applicable in non-commercial contexts as well. I experimented with these teaching techniques for years as a teacher at schools for kids between seven and sixteen years old. It's not unusual that kids too are not always equipped with tons of patience when it comes to focus and concentration and I learned how I could focus on their inner state at a certain moment in time and bring them on this teaching and learning journey that I built on The Executive Short Summary Format, Perspective Towers, Zoom-in-Zoom-out etc. These were highly appreciated techniques for some types of lessons. Then the public school as a whole is so much more than just the micro-presentation moments, it is also about experimentations, tasks, groups, programs etc.

This book about The Cassiopeia Method could only aspire to inspire teachers for certain moments during a normal school day, and those moments might do well with inspiration from more distilled commercial-based teaching.

PHILOSOPHY OF CUSTOMER EXPERIENCE

The French philosopher Jean-Paul Sartre (1905-1980) was like a walking definition of an intellectual person. He provided arguments for all kinds of versions of rationalism; like defining love and relationships. But as he got older he became very interested in *phenomenology* in which he found out that everything is not only about analytical philosophy but also *experience*. Driven by the German philosopher Edmund Husserl (1859-1938). I see a direct connection to today's way of approaching and considering a customer, with a history and present time filled with rationalism connected to price, quality, logistics, business value etc. And now this huge revelation of Customer Experience, CX, and the acknowledgement of emotions in combination with the rational factors and also the level of expectations. And then I am happy to also draw a line and link to my favorite philosopher, Danish Soren Kierkegaard (1813-1855), who highlighted the *whole* human being, he tried to paint a holistic picture of a person with freedom to choose. New thoughts back in the day of Kierkegaard's community but today highly applicable to the new customer situation with all the freedom to pick any vendor you desire.

A few other philosophers have also tried to define and describe the term *intuition*, the ability to understand something instinctively, without the need for conscious reasoning. I believe this is the case many times in Customer Experience situations, when a customer cannot always describe why they are having a great experience, but they can instinctively feel it. A great example is when you know and sense that you are having a superior experience as a customer, but it is not always easy to describe exactly why. After various interactions or touchpoints during a customer journey the sum of all the parts in combination with the expectations could end up with a thumbs up or down despite a lack of detailed analysis, it is just an intuitive conclusion based on experience, emotions and facts. This is why I keep coming back to the conclusion that it is time to leave manipulation behind and seek genuine good intent when approaching a customer. With the teaching factor of The Cassiopeia Method as the basis, to truly establish trustworthiness.

The effect and result of that aspect of Education-Based Marketing and Commercial Teaching done with The Cassiopeia Method is a great Customer Experience, CX.

This CX-value has become more and more important, even *essential*. As the unique differentiator, since almost everything else is the same between competitors, Customer Experience has risen to the top of prioritized areas for leaders in Marketing, Sales and Customer Service.

My personal experience is that when you provide humble Education-Based Marketing and Commercial Teaching with quality, making a person understand a complicated and important part of a topic, then it is like great thankfulness and openness ensues and in a customer and vendor relationship you enter a new level of respect. Many times, it creates a sense of enhanced loyalty and almost like the customer wants to pay back and return the gratitude. They might not buy from you, there are always many factors contributing to that decision, but at least they could open up and share more about themselves, their situations and unique challenges, all that you ask for as a vendor during the early stages of a Marketing and Sales process.

To sum up my philosophical approach to Customer Experience and The Cassiopeia Method I see how this approach to a customer could be one of the most important actions towards creating a unique relationship that could be both long and loyal. The reason is that if you have a long-term perspective on what you are doing with some version of Education-Based Marketing and keep providing and offering new teaching, the students and customers will come back to you.

You should become the source-to-go-to when it comes to learning and understanding a certain topic, and hopefully also encourage them to become a profitable customer, but that you need to let the customer decide.

THE CROWN JEWEL – THE INSPIRED AND TRANSFORMATIONAL CUSTOMER

There is this moment or result you want to achieve, and since you don't do manipulation the feeling will be genuine and great. All the work you spend on creating high-quality service in teaching a customer, how do you know when it is a success? How do you measure that you have achieved what you set up as an objective?

After the teaching session, no matter the format, when a customer is convinced enough to act and wants to take the next steps in the direction of engaging more in your topic, your product or your company, then you know you have succeeded with this initiative of The Cassiopeia Method.

Essentially, you have initiated a transformational process with the customer and student. You have lit a candle, you have brought enlightenment to a non-educated house. Ultimately the student states something like *finally I actually understand what this is about, now I am ready to look further into this because I understand it would be valuable for us.* Or they come to the conclusion, based on understanding, that the topic, product or you are not the solution to their problems, which is also commercially positive for you because then you can quickly qualify them out of further Sales and Marketing initiatives, at least for the time being.

How about measurements?

There are two obvious parts you can highlight and work with; first you want to have acknowledgement that the customer has reached a new level of understanding, and that can easily be done through a survey. There could be situations where you actually test the student and force them to prove they have really understood, and this is more easily done with outspoken students but doesn't always come naturally in a more formal vendor-customer relationship. The second way of measuring is to understand how empowered the customer has become to act. Either the probability of action or the actual action is the next step in the right direction taken shortly after consuming what you have provided with The Cassiopeia Method. The next steps in the Sales funnel, and that could be a booked F2F meeting with Sales, or downloading more information, or it could be signing up on an event etc. It is basically an action to engage more, and that action you can register and measure.

To be able to measure what we do is crucial in the reality in which we live, and it is best to just make it happen, although personally I would always want to highlight *the moment* it is all about – when the student "gets it", when the bits and pieces make sense and he or she (finally) understands. And you preferable see it with your own eyes, sense it. That is a great experience! And additionally, you have shed light and done something good in the world. You are part of a movement that is doing good things for customers!

CHAPTER FOUR – The Teachurator Concept

The Cassiopeia Method is a distinct and tangible method for how to explain a complicated matter in a fairly quick way. With the use of a short Executive Summary Format and other techniques I have outlined in the previous chapter.

Useful in customer-facing situations, but you could also take this even further.

With the Cassiopeia Method as the basis and best practice you could build up an Authority Character. You or someone else could take this all the way to becoming a expert in the niche of your chosen topic. That would be a person living this practice. A combination of a Teacher and a Digital Curator. I give this combination a separate professional title that of a *Teachurator*. A play with words but indeed two appreciated capabilities in a world of limited time and mental bandwidth. Living the practice of the Cassiopeia Method and/or similar approaches and ways of establishing an authoritative voice in the world. And at the same time acting as a role model on the tone, character and content-wise approach towards a modern customer dialogue, how you communicate with value, offering wisdom to share. A Teachurator should not be a one-way megaphone. Quite the opposite; through a receptive and listening mood comes an adaptive and customized approach to the customer and student. Be humble and practice authority at the same time. Teach in the conversation and be an active part of the movement towards a beautiful and new customer dialogue.

NICHE AUTHORITY IN ACTION

Different approaches in different contexts.

For some companies, it might be suitable and valuable to actually integrate The Cassiopeia Method in one or a couple of human bodies. Decide on who exactly should be *The Teacher* for the market place and customers. Who wants to be the face and the expert? The person who becomes the niche authority that customers listen to because the teaching is not directly selling or pitching per se, it is a person you can go to, listen to, and consume value from without the negative feeling of being used or sold to.

That person, or persons, should then obviously and firstly become the great modern teacher, but as we have learned in previous chapters that will not be enough, it takes more. The teacher, building an audience, also needs to see and hear the latest news, updates and thrive on insights and analysis. This means that this person also needs skills as a *Digital Curator*, as described earlier in this book. But basically you engage, mostly digitally, in your niche in the world, you establish relationships and find trustworthy data sources and communicate this. It is a great practice to implement some daily or weekly habits where you check your sources for new information, digest it, add value to it, often as shorter or longer insights, analyses, and then you share it socially in a global digital environment.

Come out of the shadows and expose yourself as an authority and voice in the market place. Become relevant and some others will want to follow you and listen to you. If you then also add modern and effective teaching skills, these combined skills could take you a long way. When I played with the wording of those two roles or skills, Teacher and Digital Curator, I came up with the new word and term *Teachurator*. It might not show up on any top list of great words, it's artificial, but at least it does the job of describing the role and position the two roles integrated into one become. A *Teachurator* is for the most part not a new role, just the term, you have seen it here and there over the last couple of years with various descriptions like Subject Matter Expert (SME), or Influencer, or Authority, or just Digital Curator.

Nevertheless, I would like to point out that most of the persons I have listened to or followed in those roles would have become even more impressive with improved teaching skills covering the whole topic and not only the pitching, piling up sales arguments of the topic. Yes, too many subjective opinions trying to win the listener over and too little real knowledge being teach.

I even believe in contributing to a better world with honest and holistic Teachurators, acting with the intent to teach and share their latest knowledge and insights from their specialty. Be the light bearer of the new enlightenment!

We are at the same time aware of the fact that those persons are often being paid or sponsored by a brand, but that is fine as long as I am not being sold to, or forced to believe in the subjective arguments from that particular person in the context of teaching or sharing digital curation.

The work of a Teachurator will help you win the authority over the global niche and create the audience group, picking up followers who eventually have a positive effect on the sales and revenue or even become the main source of new leads.

A TEACHURATOR – A TEACHER AND A DIGITAL CURATOR

A Teachurator is a person telling us new stories. Spreading enlightenment. Clarifying.

We already have that kind of person.

The new part of this is more *how* the Teachurator does it.

All the techniques within The Cassiopeia Method incorporated. Stories in Short Executive Summary Format. A true educational practice, the objective being to make people understand. And to save people time and effort when staying updated in all kinds of important topic areas. A teaching method starting with the student, the listener, the customer, the consumer and understanding the mental starting point and bring them on a learning Story Journey, no matter whether it is seconds, minutes or years.

Stories as painted pictures, complexity made simple, arising from infinite data and information, blurred by technology and difficult to catch because of speed. Confusion becomes clear with the Teachurator practice and what is presented and communicated is understandable, entertaining and done in a respectfully short format.

As stated, the Teachurator is the symbiosis of a Digital Curator and a Teacher.

Not only with words, but more interesting is the skills that come with the role.

First it is crucial to fundamentally understand what a Digital Curator does, I have touched on this in various parts of the book, such as the first part of the Cassiopeia Method that I call the Content Basis. I assume you already have a good picture of what a Teacher does, at least the traditional one, but a Digital Curator is a fairly new role and arises from a combination of art history and an exploding digital and social web.

A classic or traditional Curator is normally found in the context of a museum and is responsible for the art treasures, owning the background, the knowledge, being the content expert, a source of information and knowledge about the artistic creations. They are the single source of expertise in the area of the collections of art. Covering most or all aspects of knowledge and ownership, and a Curator is a person with deep knowledge within a niche.

More recently, the same type of character has arisen in the new tech- and media savvy world. In times of globalization and real-time it is impossible for every one of us to keep updated, follow and understand every aspect and part of the new high speed universe of modern man.

We need people who cover different areas and niches. People who own their territory, who keep track of everything that happens and are able to *curate* the most important parts and distribute the information to the rest of us. Digital Curators often distribute their concentrated information assets through social media, blogs and email lists. They play an important role for all of us to keep up without having to be all over the place ourselves.

The Teacher on the other hand is already known and appreciated as one of the most important, and underestimated professions we have. Few others have the true skill to, in a trustworthy, clear and an effective way, make sure that their students really understand and are able to act on new knowledge. The profession of a good Teacher should be elevated to the top status and treated with more respect, my opinion.

Indeed, we have seen an ongoing change in the Teacher's role, from being a preacher to become more of an orchestrator. But most important, I would argue, is the magical medicine we call the *pedagogic approach* or process of presenting a topic that every Teacher has (or should have), and it come in all colors. I teach you *my* proven and modern pedagogic process in this book, that is obviously the Cassiopeia Method.

The need for someone to be there, to stand up, explain and clarify, calmly and securely, increases in a world of companies with complex offerings and technology built into literarily everything. The world consists of fast-moving situations and it has become crucial to have someone who can manage and additionally has the ability to describe how you should relate to them. That kind of person is hugely valuable in times of extreme change and times of extreme freedom of choice. The information explosion and number of alternatives in front of us in every decision is overwhelming. Wouldn't it be helpful to have someone who can keep up, review the limitless information and present it in a pedagogic, understandable, educational way, easy to consume, in a short format?

The combination of a Digital Curator and a Teacher – a Teachurator.

Incarnated in one human being.

Or why not as an Artificial Intelligence service? See the next chapter.

For a company or organization, the Teachurator could be used by the Marketing department as a frontline spokesperson explaining to and teaching the customer audience, attracting them, creating followers just as all the other marketing assets or activities and at the end of the day, generate new businesses and customer satisfaction and loyalty.

Or, a Teachurator could be any Sales representative, incarnated as a new and appreciated way of interacting with their customers. To ensure and focus on delivering value and creating trust. A potential competitive advantage.

However, a Teachurator is not only a play on words, it is the formalization of a role we have partly seen before, but now, with this new set of tools, with new approaches to clarify what is complex and with a condensed set of digital curation and teaching skills and effective communication principles defined – becomes the standard-bearer of the new Enlightenment.

A Teachurator in action knows how to present complex information effectively and understandably.

But how, more specifically, does a Teachurator act and work?

Apart from the Cassiopeia Methods, built up of three main parts; the Content Basis, the Look and the Story Journey, I would suggest also looking at the Teachurator practice as three processes leading up to the expected concept of a Teachurator. Similar or the same as the Cassiopeia Method but also a way of creating a complete picture of the Teachurator practice and getting even closer to the essence of that profession.

First: *The Digital Curator process.* The Teachurator acts as a Digital Curator, learns how to find and dig up important information, news, trends, pros and cons, tangible examples, background, notices significant industry actors in the niche. Learns how to identify trustworthy sources of information, knows how to grasp the information, structure it, understand and analyze what is important and not. It is also crucial to learn how to share the information and the insights during this process, because giving and sharing is a great way of ensuring recognition and getting information in return from other actors in the niche bubble.

Second: *The Teacher's pedagogic process,* to create a pedagogic (make sure the receiver understands) approach. Think and act as a teacher and a student, build up a journey for the students, a mental road to walk, a pedagogic communication picture, consumable in parts and ultimately painting the big picture.

Third: *The Teachurator process.* Put it all together; the Digital Curator and Teacher skills and add a few new Teachurator practices. Those parts could be the presentation format, the crystal-clear mental journey, aligned to a new world and new needs of the audience. The format needs to be short, distilled, every word must carry value, it must be pedagogic and entertaining. The expectations are high, standards are high, it is not easy to be or become an appreciated Teachurator. The Teachurator presents in a Short Executive Summary Format, the receiver is basically short of time and mental bandwidth.

FOR CHANGE MANAGEMENT AND COMMUNICATION TOO

The Cassiopeia Method is valuable and useful for customer-facing professionals like Sales, Consultants and Customer Support to establish trust, as well as within the practice of Content- or Education-Based Marketing for a marketing department.

Although, it doesn't need to stop there.

The potential is broader. What if more people within the company, if not all, started acting as within the concepts and techniques of the Cassiopeia Method?

Internal Communication.

Managers.

The Cassiopeia Method could be an effective tool when implementing Change Management within a company. Or at least influence the communication part of the Change Management process. To explain the complexities, to be crystal clear on what will happen, to educate on what is new and what is coming. When conducting transformation programs to help employees understand and get faster into their new position by teaching them the correct state of mind and skill. A *Train the Trainer* principle, because when you need to teach something you increase your ability to learn it yourself. And the positive effects from an educational approach in a Change Management process are that the organization is more aware and has a better understanding, the change tends to be more positive and effective, in contrast to not understanding or just being informed. The Cassiopeia Method as an internal tool and enabler might be provide underestimated potential to see a positive change or at least reduce the negative challenges that can easily occur during a change process.

The Cassiopeia Method in its essence is a modern educational communication process.

Applicable in multiple use cases.

The need for clarification and enlightenment in short and effective formats is easy to identify. My prediction is that this need will continue to grow and the practice of good teaching becomes even more important, in many areas.

CHAPTER FIVE: The Beauty of Technology and KPIs

OUR NEW BINARY BODY, BLOOD AND INNOVATION

When Technology is like magic it is at its best.

But many times, we perceive Technology differently.

It's unfair when some subjects in our world might come in more or less strict packages and also might appear to be a bit boring, and even cold and mechanical. That could be the case for subjects like Economics, Law or Science in general. Just like Technology. But it's mostly about how the subjects are presented and not wrapped in a nice exciting present you can't wait until you open. There are endless thrilling opportunities to explore. Technology stands out because it's closely linked to *innovation*. Or the opportunity to shape and design the future.

The subject of *art* is normally associated with paintings, music and literature – the creation of something we've never seen or experienced before. People thinking outside the box, pushing the boundaries, provocative, exploring new frontiers for your mind and emotions. Unfortunately, Technology is rarely mentioned as part of the world of art. Probably because most of the art coming out from the world of Technology is also required to be useful. And that could be a tough requirement for a classical *artist*.

Technological innovation. The intersection between Technology and Creation.

This is interesting, because when we look back in history we can treat groundbreaking innovations as natural and maybe not as re-markable as they were at that time. We tend to soon forget how it was just before and how limited our minds were before. Conse-quently, it's the same situation now, as probably the case in most *now* situations, when we are looking ahead and we have huge difficulties seeing what's coming because of our limited minds. It's hard, and it's an art to be able to think outside the box, to visualize, to solve a problem in the world without any believers or anyone that sees how it could be.

A few examples.

The car, with the famous quote by the inventor of the T-Ford car, Henry Ford (1863-1947): "If I had asked people what they wanted, they would have said *faster horses*."

In the 16th century most people and institutions believed the Earth was the fixed center of the Universe, but Nicolaus Copernicus (1473-1543) dared to challenge that and proposed the theory of the Sun being in the center of the planets and that the Earth rotates on its own axis, a heliocentric world. He made the observations only with his eyes, no telescopes! You might want to define this as a discovery rather than innovation, but it's quite related. The openness for new possibilities.

The smartphone. Maybe you take a multi-functional device for granted nowadays, but when the first smartphones were presented in 2006-2007 there were many completely negative expert comments and skepticisms. Search for videos with comments connected to the legendary days of the announcement of the first versions of smartphones. And then think about how that device completely disrupted a whole industry. Actually, many industries. The world.

If there is one area in the aspects of modern Technology that I would choose to highlight, it needs to be *software*. It is the core of most new innovation these days. With software, you can create almost any kind of service or product. And it is at the core of what is rising fast with Artificial Intelligence, AI. But those areas can easily be very complicated and the need for people who can explain, describe and outline functionality, value and deployment is huge.

This is why the (Software) Technology revolution goes hand in hand with Education-Based Marketing, Commercial Teaching and most aspects of Content Marketing. And consequently, the practice of the Cassiopeia Method. People want to understand! And Technology is in general complicated.

We live in a powerful era of Technology.

Technology implicates most parts of our lives and companies. We need help to keep up. We need help to understand.

I argue that we have never lived in a time with a greater need for the voice of a Teacher, clarifying and spreading enlightenment. A most relevant and appreciated force and value-add in our lives.

ROBO-TEACHER AS A SYMBOL

Technology development is exploding and a delicate matter to address since it will soon become outdated.

But I recommend bookmarking information sources for Educational Technology (EdTech), Marketing Technology (MarTech) and CRM (Customer Relationship Management) with connections to Artificial Intelligence (AI).

And robots.

It's such a declarative picture, a robot acting as a teacher, or a customer representative.

I assume a common initial reaction to the role of the teacher would be, it's never going to work. It's too complicated a situation to manage for a robot. The teaching situation.

Personally, I have learned to not adopt too binary a perspective when it comes to potential future scenarios. Many times, in unbelievable scenarios, innovation and Technology together with the human being find a way forward and it all ends up in reasonable and balanced solutions.

Obviously, I don't know anything about the future, but I do see the potential of using Technology for education and teaching in ways we haven't seen or done before.

I remember my days as a teacher in public schools for children between eight and sixteen and although I am now an optimistic Technology futurist I will be more than impressed the day I look into a classroom and I see a robot taking care of all the chaotic interactions, emotions, special needs, hidden agendas and pranks. But there could be other applications, not least as an *assistant* to the human teacher or a *special topic teacher*, giving lectures in very specific topics. Because there is at least one huge upside when considering the machine vs human being – the machine has potentially instant access to gigantic sources of information. And also, it could have an increased capacity to draw conclusions and make sense out of all the data there is. Gathering all relevant data, digging Big Data, applying Artificial Intelligence like Machine Learning, Deep

Learning and Natural Language Processing (NLP). If we could also teach the machine and robot to holistically see and understand the individual student, and customize the Story Journey then we could probably make a lot of use of this new teacher.

Although I love the picture of a classic metal and plastic robot on wheels in a classroom, talking like machines do in movies, I believe the teaching tech assistants are more likely to appear in other formats; on the devices we use, individually or as a group, or as a humanoid on the screen.

Nevertheless, how about a robot version of a Teachurator? For the Marketing department?

We have already seen robots becoming technical writers and even act as journalists. What's stopping the development from creating a robot that is highly skilled in all the teaching tactics I share in this book? Not much, I assume. And we see already today all kinds of initiatives and products coming up.

But how to create and establish trust in a robot and what human being does really want to follow a machine?

Probably more people than you might think. Again, this doesn't need to be either or. And in the context of customers and business: is the customer really that concerned about who to follow as long as it solves their immediate problems?

Personally, I believe there is still an arena for and high value in being a human being, at least in our most immediate future. To manage all kind of levels of human communication, body language, complicated natural language, empathy, reading and interpreting emotions, adapting to specific needs students etc. And so-called *Educational Cobots* – working *with* humans rather than replacing them would potentially provide a great upside for a modern teacher. A winning team.

The Robo-Teacher. Welcome.

Could we also see *new teaching methods* by a Robo-Teacher? Ways of teaching we have never seen before? Never thought of? This is interesting!

Since they could potentially have instant access to all the data in the world, what if we found a way to use real-time sources? That could become the most knowledgeable teacher in the world. But would it automatically become the best teacher by knowledge only? No, it takes more. Here we have the pedagogical part, and the empathy, the understanding of an individual human being.

Obviously, I speculate in this chapter since we don't know where the future will take us, but fast development is happening, it is probably not long before we'll see new product solutions at scale. And it might be that Robo-Teachers become the specialists that a company or school hires. Different robots for different topics and we let them teach their topic, like a specific language or a specific technology. *The Teaching Specialist Robot.*

Could we develop a robot service that creates great Executive Short Summary formats of any topic? Based on access to Big Data, Artificial Intelligence (AI), Machine Learning, Deep Learning etc. Could we create a standard format that is likely to be understood of most people?

Could we map out a format for the perfect best practice of the Cassiopeia Method built on a short, summarized format, with a journey, a standardized start and probable good repetition stops? Could this be done effectively without the acknowledgement signals from the student? Or why not built-in acknowledgements? Without adapting to the changing state of mind of the student? Yes, I think we could.

Hey, Technology entrepreneurs, I just gave you something to work on!

VIRTUAL SKY IS THE LIMIT

If we leave robots and science fiction teaching for a while and focus on concrete Technology for a human teacher, customer-facing professionals, a Teachurator and Marketing department there are a few areas where help can be provided.

I will not give guidance on specific technology products in this book, I leave that to updated blog posts, news and community forums.

But let's match the Cassiopeia Method to Technology on a high level.

Part 1 – The Content Basis.

Research, analyze and clarify through information gathering, the collection of data. Tools for Digital Curation; through Web, Social Media listening Technology, Big Data, AI, Machine Learning, Deep Learning. There are many ways to track and use flags on updates and follow hashtags, topics and news. Also, tools for gathering and categorizing important information, links and various media content.

Part 2 – The Look.

Using tools that know how to gather all the relevant data about a student and customer. Everything from attributes to behaviors and needs and context data. Like a Data Marketing Platform (DMP). 360 view of the customer technology, CRM-systems (Customer Relationship Management), Personalization Tools etc.

Part 3 – The Story Journey.

Distribution of insights and teaching to the audience. Through sharing, create awareness, build an audience. Publication, Marketing clouds/platforms, get the message out there, EdTech, Online Education, portals. Understand the student, see the student, helping tools, personalization, real time.

More about the crucial part of The Look.

And the challenge that every human being on this earth is unique.

And every exact moment in time is also unique. A huge challenge for both technology and us to address. Let me give an example. Coffee.

It's important to me. Well, maybe not as serious as life or death (although I sometimes think it might be), but coffee means a lot to me anyway. I appreciate a cup when I wake up, ground whole beans with a little heated milk, but it's mostly because I have access to an excellent coffee machine. It could have worked out just as well if I served myself with plain brewed coffee, but then it's not given that I prefer milk in the cup. Sometimes milk in brewed coffee is good but just as often a classic cup of black coffee is perfectly fine. When I visit a coffee house I tend to order a small latte with an extra espresso shot, flat white, and when I am really tired I'll have three shots in it. When that is not served, I'll go for an ordinary café latte, but please, not too much foam, preferably just a little cream. At work, I drink any kind of coffee, it could come from a standard vending machine, no problem, but I appreciate finer coffee and strong small latte, cappuccino, and plain brewed coffee in that order. But yes, sometime after lunch a macchiato can be nice. On a weekend night, after a dinner with everything that goes with it, well, I prefer a double espresso.

How could marketers in combination with technology at a coffee company calculate what I want and need? How can companies that sell coffee products and services analyze and map my behavior, needs and desires and align their products to just me, to personalize? How can a computer possibly understand me? How can they align their marketing and sales activities to me, see me, and set the right journey in motion?

And that is just me.

One human being among a billion others.

About coffee. Think about adding all other areas of interest; how I take care of my car, buy food, clothes and manage bank matters. Or, by all means, all the complex procurement events and processes in the Business-to-Business (B2B) context.

Companies build departments, with people, technology and data, wholly dedicated to reading patterns down to the individual person, in order to align the Customer eperience to a journey and all its unique situations.

It's an ambitious aspiration.

To some extent it's already there and working, but it is probably safe to say that we can expect some exciting developments in a sophisticated direction. Today it's called personalization or contextualization, tomorrow we might call it something else. But it is about a human being, a small dot on the map, that we put in the center. It is that individual that every company wants to get on the hook. And take care of, as a customer-obsessed company. Like the Teacher in the classroom seeing all the unique students sitting there in chairs looking inspired, tired, concentrated, dreaming etc. Many times, it is fairly easy for the Teacher to read the behaviors of the individuals in the class. In more of a mass-market model, or at least when you have the ambition to reach thousands and millions of students or customers you probably need help, and that help comes partly from Technology. Most tools and innovative approaches seem to be accepted, the only limitation as it appears could be the person itself, putting their foot down, saying no thank you.

And the main reason for this to happen could be that customers are tired of being *manipulated*. They don't appreciate the feeling of someone working on you, selling to you, trying to lure you, argument with and convince you, track you and explain to you without you giving them your permission to give you advice.

The human being has a well explored part of the body, the amygdala, that is the center of fear control, a function that is always on, 24*7, looking for danger around us. That part of us is an expert at detecting manipulation. And the reaction is to flee or to fight. We just don't appreciate being manipulated.

Technology is the big enabler and empowerment tool that make this all so much more interesting because of the ability to reach out and build customer audiences globally. The democratization of technology, low barriers of entry, makes it interesting and essential for all companies.

MEASUREMENTS OF UNDERSTANDING

The balance and combination of open, trustworthy teaching with business focus could be a challenge if you are not crystal clear on the measurements.

At the end of the day the Cassiopeia Method is not primarily a community service, the reason for doing this is to be commercially effective, creating trust and higher customer satisfaction.

The commercial dimension, how does it affect the design and actual execution of the practice of the Cassiopeia Method? Then we are back to the smaller and larger business objectives, strategies, followers and branding. What kind of customer-facing professional or company do you want to be? Just the fact that you are doing this, providing instant value in the form of education, puts you in a new light. But also, the other way around, the brand you want to be affects the *tone* of your teaching style. For example, there's a huge difference in character and brand when you compare one company that acts in the innovation frontier of their industry wanting to explore new territories and a completely different company that is more conservative and sticks to what the industry has learnt from experience and focuses on the later phases or even after market. The first company obviously needs to be more visionary but also be sure they don't lose the customer, and the second company need to pay attention to the details for optimizing and being even more efficient. And those two approaches affect the educational and communicational style very much. To challenge the customer or not is another example.

It has to be crystal clear where the company is in terms of: company culture and brand, the company strategy and not least the concrete objectives for a specific product or area of interest for the specific educational approach. What do you want to achieve? Is it higher customer satisfaction and/or to find new business opportunities and/or to help potential customers in their buying journey to move forward and/or increase loyalty and/or market a new category and simply educate a new market connected to the company's future strategy.

The reasons for applying The Cassiopeia Method could be many, what is important is that the individual professional and company are crystal clear on why they do what they do. And this need to be measured in order to see what is effective and what is not. You might be acting in a market where the customers tend to not look at videos for inspiration or education, they prefer to meet in-person or go on an event, then you need see that reflected in your numbers. Or if you are aiming to apply the Cassiopeia Method for global Marketing and everything you do needs to be digital and you have no idea what tools and channels that are most effective, then you need to set up a measurement system in order to make solid business decisions over time based on previous results. That is no different from the other tactics within Marketing, Sales and Communication. Let me highlight a couple of KPIs (Key Performance Indicator) for the work you aspire to do with the Cassiopeia Method.

I divide them into primary and secondary measurements, where primary KPIs are the immediate effect you want to achieve and secondary KPIs are the subsequent value drivers for the business.

Primary; Trust, Customer Satisfaction, Engagement.

Secondary; Audience growth, Loyalty, Leads, Opportunities, Pipeline, Qualification, Type/format of the Cassiopeia Method delivery.

I prefer to think of the Cassiopeia Method as a growth driver, a method for *increasing* vital business aspects. At the end of the day, a revenue driver. Financially, companies are all about changing a number of KPIs to increase the revenue, and decrease the cost and then obviously calculate a summarized positive profit. I know there are alternative business models, especially in the startup context, but basically that description goes for most companies and the Cassiopeia Method is mainly meant to contribute to increasing various parts of the revenue side of the calculation.

How could you measure ROI (Return On Investment) using the Cassiopeia Method?

Well, of course you can measure how much time and how much of your financial resources you have invested in enabling your organization and teaching it how to apply the Cassiopeia Method. Then you can look at the current business status and track the changes in revenue, business pipeline, customer satisfaction index etc. and connect the results to the investment and look at the changes and through classic calculation see where the breakeven is. However, the Cassiopeia Method is just one skill and practice among quite a lot of other parameters in a Sales, Marketing and Services business. It's not a credible calculation. It's better to stick to the concrete KPIs mentioned above and follow up through surveys after customer meetings for customer satisfaction indication, and then look at the other measurements with a humble and holistic analytical eye.

Obviously, there is Technology for all the measurement aspects; to collect data, analyze and report. Surveys as digital and automated and Sales, Marketing and Services metrics traced within with organization as usual with all available tools for Customer Management Relationship (CRM), Marketing Automation, and Service Dashboards.

ALGORITHMS IN THE NEW CUSTOMER DIALOGUE

It goes without saying that this book needs some content that explains a few of the most outstanding capabilities aspiring to strongly influence the future development of new services. The reason I'm including it in this book is the clear trend that most parts of the Cassiopeia Method and this New Customer Dialogue will be empowered and absorbed by various new algorithms, services, products and developments within Artificial Intelligence (AI). *Machines communicating directly with the customer, in a dialogue format.* Stay tuned is my recommendation, here's just an explanatory introduction, it doesn't even scrape the surface:

Artificial Intelligence.
The term says a lot. It is constructed intelligence, meaning that we are to some extent trying to copy human intelligence, and even improve it. The obvious first question mark is, what is intelligence? The traditional definition of *intelligence* is about *the ability to acquire and apply knowledge and skills.* By that we learn there are two parts to intelligence, one concerns acquiring data, information, knowledge and skills and the other concerns applying it. To create an artificial version of intelligence you need to master both those two sides, to begin with. The first aspect, about the acquirement, embraces a machine's capability to read natural language, (as one example,) which in itself is a complicated challenge since words and sentences can mean different things depending on the context, consequently this makes demands on a lot of knowledge beyond simply letters and words.
Take the following famous sentence which provide challenges for a computer to understand properly: *Last night I shot an elephant in my pajamas.*
Shooting the elephant with a camera or a weapon? Who is wearing the pajamas? A computer has to look at similar sentences and information sources and then calculate options with various probabilities

of being the correct one. Or try this one: *Paris Hilton was in Paris, stayed at Hilton Paris, and listened to Paris.* As human beings, we use our memory, knowledge and experiences and draw conclusions around what a sentence *probably* means. The technological development in this area has moved fast forward, computer systems are becoming highly skilled at this. Similar work is done with sound and visual information, and other cognitive senses. One huge upside with a computer system is that it can quickly scan huge amounts of data, and since we today have *Big Data* and keep collecting new endless seas of data we become dependent on the computer systems to scan the data sources for useful information. When you then combine this with huge computational capacity and data models, sample models, prediction capabilities, trend and analytical tools, you have a natural bridge over to the part concerning how to apply the knowledge (Machine Learning). Here's where the AI-services materialize themselves in tangible services that learn something and apply it, and can do it fast, at scale and occasionally more accurately than a human being.

Within Sales, Marketing and Services we see a huge focus on *assistant services*, meaning that professionals working with customers get suggestions and advice from the AI-service about how to act in order to maximize the chances of increasing business and customer satisfaction etc. It could be about suggestions around the next few steps in a deal process, based on facts from millions of other similar deals. Or a Customer Support professional could immediately use an AI-assistant to find the most appropriate solutions for a support case. AI-services even become more and more capable of e taking care of customers independently using a speaking tool and voice recognition (Deep Learning).

And with this knowledge of what Artificial Intelligence could be we should also clearly expect interesting development within the scope of the Cassiopeia Method. The Content Basis is a job for the AI-service to take care of, the same goes for The Look, based on all potential information there is about individual persons and adding visual capabilities and the ability to read their emotions. Then we already see AI-services creating stories so why not also the

Story Journey with the ambition to teach something and do that in alignment with the student.

The hardest part, if you ask me personally, would be to read the human being, the unique individual, look into their eyes and judge where their mind and emotions are, and be able to adapt to that and being empathic. Since this is occasionally critical in order to open up a closed situation or get someone to switch perspective and prepare them for learning.

Machine Learning.

Once again, look at the words: *Machine Learning*. That's what it is, a machine trying to learn something from data and experience. There are many aspects, definitions and various applications close to Machine Learning for the scholars to debate. But just for us to understand on a high level there is one approach I'd like to provide as an example. A computer system starts by looking at a smaller sample of data and applying it to a model, it starts to adjust the variables in the model to understand potential patterns. Then it applies this to real data and analyzes how well it matches and with mathematical optimization algorithms helps the ongoing improvement until the system seems to get the model right and the pattern recognition in place. It has then "learned" the pattern, how the various data parts are related. This process could be supervised by a "teacher" or be unsupervised learning.

Think about all the use cases where we as human beings just can't figure out how complex matters work and we can instead let a machine give it a go and try to learn how it all works. Especially in our complex world of financial real-time systems, societies, countries, corporates and billions of individual human beings, all with their own agendas. No to mention, "unsolvable" problems like some severe deceases.

Machine Learning comes from the discipline of Artificial Intelligence and is often considered to be a part of AI.

Deep Learning.

Considered as part of Machine Learning and using learning representations of unstructured data, trying to model high levels of abstractions of the data. Using hierarchical representations in layers with the higher level derived from the lower level. Then the algorithms transform the input data through the various layers. This hierarchy of layers is often referred to as the notion of an artificial neural network in which we have the connection between the nervous system, human brain and body. The more abstract levels learn from the lower levels. The most famous areas for deep learning are speech recognition, image (pictures and video) recognition and natural language processing. And we see it applied within the commercial world in a number of places, like within marketing as recommendation engines suggesting related and relevant products for customers.

Looking at all this Technology I see a future with great possibilities for the Cassiopeia Method being used with different aspects of Artificial Intelligence, Educational Technology (EdTech) and Marketing Technology (MarTech). To teach the machines to behave in the new customer dialogue, to be personalized and provide valuable teaching.

Human beings are algorithms, machines are algorithms. A dialogue between whoever it might be, is multiple algorithms interacting and taking various directions during the session. Dependent factors weigh in, instant probability calculations are part of the decision making, a complex net of cause and effect. It's a fascinating scene, the dialogue, both predictable and unpredictable, a place to explore opportunities but also to risk everything. Hence, algorithms are a delicate topic, filled with hope and fear, history and future at one and the same time. Nevertheless, in its purest definition, an algorithm is described as *a procedure to solve a problem, based on conducting a sequence of specified actions*. And *solve a problem* could also be *to fulfill a need* or *to achieve something*.

The design of a dialogue keeps evolving. And when we train machines to do this well, with human beings, it reminds us of how wonderfully the human being's brain is constructed, what we can perform and how multi-faceted a communication between two people can be, the face-to-face meeting. Like the one with a customer.

Customers interact more and more with machines, the dialogue is on, and we need to ensure that machines also respect the need for The New Customer Dialogue.

Algorithms as the future magic formula are not to be underestimated, especially not in a customer dialogue context.

CHAPTER SIX: The Hunger for Clarity in Complex Industries

IT'S COMPLICATED

Let's remind ourselves of the business case for The Cassiopeia Method.

In this world there are some quite straightforward things and some parts that are pretty hard to understand.

Nevertheless, there are at least four challenges here; firstly, the topic might be too complicated to digest properly even with desire and time, or secondly you might not always be able to summon the right interest for the topic and thirdly you just don't have the time and fourthly the mental bandwidth doesn't allow for more.

And since we don't see fewer of the complicated situations connected to a decision, quite the opposite, they proliferate, this is becoming a real issue for many of us.

This is especially obvious in more complex industries. And here is the big gap I identified. It is far too common that a vendor in a complex industry just can't explain for a customer how things are working, how they are connected and what implications various decisions have.

What is then a complex industry? Of course, it could be any industry, it's up to the individual customer to judge but I would like to highlight a few obvious industries. First and foremost, I have to mention my own industry of Technology/IT/Software that is by nature a rapidly changing culture, always new versions, generations and cutting-edge technology. It is not only complicated; it is also in a high-speed situation and everything is connected and interdependent. A decision about one device or piece of software has to be related to everything it should be integrated to and work together with.

Other industries with complex product structures and confusing commercial agreements and hard to judge effects on decisions are Banking and Finance with multiple perceived complicated products with related calculated and forecasted risk. Related to this industry is Wealth and Investments. And more on the personal side is Pensions, Insurance and Energy solutions. Or why not Real Estate or Schools/ Education? What they all have in common is that they demand important decisions with significant implications and they all need extra commitment to understand and prepare for making good decisions.

This is where an approach from vendors with the Cassiopeia Method is very much needed. And appreciated.

Trust is the common theme; that is what makes the big difference. Trust is the new currency in a non-manipulative way; true *trust* can't exist at the same time as manipulation. Well, it can, but the moment the manipulation is exposed the trust is gone. Trust is the foundation of all genuine businesses, now it's even more important when customers are smarter than ever and have the power and the ability to move to another supplier whenever they choose to.

Although, the advent of trust as a foundation mostly comes down to our needs. We need help, and when we need help we are often exposed and vulnerable, and then even more sensitive and can "feel" trust. We appreciate help in order to create stability again and figure out how to find our own unique place, gain appreciation and enable Self- Actualization, if that is what we are aiming for. Not all people, by far, seem to be interested in that though, but there is a broad need for understanding without having time or mental bandwidth for it.

Sitting at the coffee house and looking out at sunny Stockholm, where people pass by, with music in my earphones, seeing smiling faces, sad, surprised, neutral, determined or disappointed faces. That's when I realize the world orbits around the individual human being. Every little world is part of a bigger world, a universe that expands, on its way forward, just like all these people.

The individual human being is everything. And many times, a sensitive little world.

I *see* a person in an entirely different kind of way. I see a feature film, a book series, I see a romantic story that can be anything but romantic. A human being blossoms out and then dies. But there is time in between that is valuable. Precious time.

The *value* we encounter all the time within corporates. Everyone wants to offer value to the customer. It's *business value*, customer value, value offering etc. It's easy to get caught up in the terms about value so that we almost forget what kind of value that counts the most.

The value for the individual human being.

When you have established trust the door opens and the receiver is tuned in and listens to you. Might not buy anything this time but at least you have won their attention for a moment, and that could be the start of something new.

That individual is worth great treatment, another level of service, help to make good decisions, help to understand and be confident. Trust builds on knowledge and enlightenment. In a good example, driven by the solid specialist in the industry and clarifying with simple words and a good Story Journey ending up in a positive commercial decision.

LEARNING IS ABOUT SURVIVAL AND PASSION

Universe.

Billions of stars.

Hundreds of millions of galaxies.

The sun is one star in billions, and the sun with its circulating planets is a world just in itself, complex enough.

Again, I see the connection to every human being on earth, that we can compare with a star in the universe.

Every individual person is like a mini universe. Large and complex, but in the context of a limited and small universe.

We are a couple of billions of people on earth trying to learn something. The individual human being's ability to survive is built upon learning, from younger years to older. That is one big common denominator for people. And this has become brutally apparent during modern times, when industrialism has driven urbanization with a simpler life in the countryside being replaced by a more complex life in the city, and at the same time as network technology has changed the way we looked at countries' borders and people have become global citizens, companies competing with companies all over the world. People are connected, and we are mobile and social. Technology and economics are difficult topics and hard to keep up with and follow with an acceptable level of understanding, at least to gain enough information and understanding to be able to make solid decisions. It's highly demanding to keep up, stay updated, understand and know what to do and how to act. At least concerning the more complicated matters we face. We can easily grasp the first parts, the more basic levels of information and comprehend them through googling, reading articles, blogs, being socially active and asking others for advice. But the next level, where we need to understand the hard parts, and especially in a relevant context for us specifically, then some solid, reliable and customized teaching is highly appreciated. Learning has risen in importance again and is badly needed. Information, knowledge and scientific truths are fleeting data, they come and go, change and demand you to be humble and flexible.

And for many of us, learning is so much more than just survival. It's a (great portion of) passion. A longing to understand more, get a grip of something, see the big picture, dive into details, learn enough to be able to teach.

Teaching and Learning.

Two sides of the same coin.

Learning we do for ourselves. And others. Teaching for others. And ourselves.

Learning is a part of our body, it's built in.

Teaching is something you can learn, one of the big professions. The ability to teach is a skill and art worth practicing, cultivating and promoting as one of the most important capabilities and virtues we have. To support other human beings in surviving and enriching their passions.

A LEADER TO FOLLOW

Leadership.

One topic but all the same a quality and profession we never end debating. It's constantly up for discussion and the number of suggestions on how it should be done and designed never run dry.

But the simple fact that we are social creatures in a terrain difficult to navigate, generates a constant need for leaders to follow and listen. Who detaches from the group and takes responsibility, argue about what to do, when and how, suggests direction and also suggests an answer to why a certain direction is to be preferred. The leader has a strong influence on us and there are few we appreciate as much as leaders we trust and respect. When leadership is at its strongest, vital, genuine and helpful – then I know few professions that are as impressive and important. But there are many deviations. Many times, real leadership is forgotten, too many other tasks are expected of the leader, suddenly they don't have time to practice what they should, they solely carry out management tasks instead of guiding the team. The proactive leader becomes a reactive leader with their main task being to maintain order in the organization. The leader becomes a manager. And the manager works for the organization itself, the leader works for human beings, to show the direction with a smile and say *follow me*.

Great teachers are also great leaders in the sense of their high level of influence, and the voice of a teacher with authority touches the underlying human need to follow a leader. To listen and learn from someone they trust and are willing to follow. Great teachers create a comfort zone of learning and they challenge the student to come along on an adventure, to learn new stuff, experience new things and come back as another and changed person. Great teachers are great leaders and we listen to them and happily and freely follow them.

That is the utopian application of the Cassiopeia Method; the leader and teacher guides the student and customer through the uncertain terrain and end up with clear sight and safe ground.

CHAPTER SEVEN: The Book Executive Summary

APPRECIATED TEACHING THAT CREATES SMILES OF UNDERSTANDING

Complexity is all over us; there is newly invented technology, online services, multiple choices requiring constant important personal decisions and in combination with personal limitations in time and mental bandwidth there is a great opportunity in the world for brands and passionate individuals to take on the role of a Teacher and Digital Curator and explain topics in an effective and consumable style.

Additionally, we unfortunately have a history of too much distrusted Marketing and Sales practice with ingredients of manipulation, fiddle and a content blur. There is a trust issue in times when brands are desperate for loyal customers, the global competition is harder than ever and the customers make the decisions.

The customer is expecting a new kind of dialogue. They need help to understand relevant topics in order to make good decision, solve complicated problems and they don't have time for much else. The expectations have risen and personalization is taken for granted.

The time has come for The New Customer Dialogue.

The Cassiopeia Method is one way of approaching some of these challenges.

Here are the tactics I recommend to embrace, they are all part of The Cassiopeia Method; expectation management, executive summary format, story journeys, zoom in and zoom out, instructional teaching vs perspective teaching, in-flow-repetition, the Swedish perspective, humor, perspective towers, play intelligence, digital curation and application of the Teachurator concept.

The Cassiopeia Method consists of three simple parts;

- The Content Basis
- The Look
- The Story Journey

Make this an integrated skill for you and your colleagues with one-on-one customer meetings, and also let content marketers learn how to apply this in educational content creation and interactions.

The Cassiopeia Method is a reminder to stay with the customer, and during the customer journey, to lead them through the process and journey instead of just pointing to a vision and hoping that they will eventually "get it". Instead, be an active guide and provide constant value, during all steps moving forward. You will probably get the dopamine kick when the customer and student pays you with an understanding smile. Done well you build a foundation of Trust that most of the times should bring you a commercial positive upside.

Sales representatives, Marketers and Consultants – consider yourself Teachers, but please avoid just preaching and pitching. Instead, communicate in a dialogue, and with finesse. Don't take yourself too seriously, use good humor, warm empathy and become a trusted guide all the way to the higher level of understanding.

"Education is the kindling of a flame, not the filling of a vessel."
Socrates

Exactly what the Cassiopeia Method should be about, to drive enlightenment!

To shine as a star. Be a star. A Cassiopeia Star.

Together with your Customer, you form the Customer Dialogue making it something beautiful and bright: a star constellation. Remember that in your next customer meeting and you are part of the movement of a beautiful and new Customer Dialogue with personalization and teaching.